# COLOR TV STUDIO DESIGN & OPERATION:
## for CATV, School, & Industry

### By Oliver Berliner

**TAB BOOKS**

Blue Ridge Summit, Pa. 17214

FIRST EDITION

FIRST PRINTING—APRIL 1975

Copyright © by TAB BOOKS

Printed in the United States
of America

Hardbound Edition: International Standard Book No. 0-8306-4755-4

Library of Congress Card Number: 74-14329

## *About This Book*

We wish to acknowledge the cooperation of *Broadcast Management/Engineering* and *TV Communications* in helping to make this book possible. Mr. Berliner originally wrote this book as a series of articles published in these magazines.

Other than slight alterations to titles and minor text changes, no attempt has been made to change the essential magazine article style in which the text was first written.

Publishers

## *About The Author*

Oliver Berliner is an audioman who turned to video prior to the color era. He was a kinescope recording engineer for NBC before the advent of video tape recorders. A cofounder of the Audio Engineering Society, he is also a member of NCTA and SMPTE. His interest in audio stemmed from the fact that his grandfather, the late Emile Berliner, is the inventor of the microphone, disc record, and disc record player. As president of Soundesign Consulting Engineers of Beverly Hills and Telaudio Centre Distributing of Burbank, the author put the firms heavily into video in 1966. He is familiar with every aspect of TV studio design from the standpoints of the engineer, the architect, and the producer.

# Contents

# Chapter 1

# The Multiple Studio—
# Designing the Building

This book explores in detail everything management and the chief engineer must know in connection with the creation and technical operation of a television show production facility. There are, in effect, three kinds of studios—and each will be carefully examined—the elaborate plant encompassing more than one studio, the single but complete studio layout, and the budget-conscious array—in that order.

Hopefully, one or more of these plans will meet the reader's requirements, or he may wish to combine certain distinct features of each. Everything in this book will be directed towards the CATV, industrial, and educational user.

It may become evident that many of the things proposed herein are not inexpensive. This is true, for when we say "low cost" we mean in comparison to a facility using broadcast-grade cameras and video tape recorders. (All equipment described will, however, border on broadcast versatility and quality—but at a fraction of the customary cost to the broadcaster.)

In the portion covering studios, fixed or mobile, it will be assumed that their primary function is for the making of videotapes for playback elsewhere or later. While attention will be given to production that is being transmitted live to the viewers, such as in a cable TV or instructional situation, it must first be established that the television networks long ago realized that prerecording is the best way to properly and economically use the studios while simultaneously obtaining more-perfect programs, artistically and technically.

Today, there is very little live programming on the air; what little we see is mostly news and sports. Consequently, our studio designs and equipment selection and connection will be in keeping with this style of operation, although live distribution will be provided for and will be discussed later.

Everything considered will be with respect to color television. This book will not, however, deal heavily with studio lighting because, although critical in color TV, it has been often and amply covered before. One further word of explanation is needed: Each chapter of this book will at one time or another mention matters requiring explanation. When such is necessary but not given, it is because that subject has been, or will be, covered in detail elsewhere in the book. Please be patient in this respect.

### The Workable Layout

There is much more to a television production facility than just a studio and control room—as many users have learned too late. It is in reality the *supporting areas* and their placement which make for smooth production.

Since few CATV (or other nonbroadcast facility) arrays dictate more than a two-studio setup, an elaborate layout containing one audience studio and a nonaudience studio (although portable bleacher seats may be installed in the nonaudience acting area) will be described.

It is recommended that the reader who is contemplating construction of a sophisticated teleproduction plant visit a commercial television station to study their floor plan and the facilities needed to complement the studios themselves.

### The Complete Building

Figure 1-1 shows a suggested layout. While the reader may be surprised at many of the things found here, such things as closets, commissary, power service entrance, lighting and camera equipment storage, and other things the commercial stations often require, some of which you will want to include—have been omitted.

A complete headquarters building is shown—including offices and studios. Some of the hallways are wider than others so that equipment can easily be moved from place to place—including from studio to remote van when parked in the street or at the loading dock; the latter is covered so that equipment may be placed there in the rain and sets may be moved from the construction/storage area into Studio B.

Yes, a set and props construction area is one of the things frequently overlooked, along with the men's and women's dressing rooms. Note how access to the lavatories is obtained both from the dressing rooms and without having to go through them. The latter is for the convenience of technical personnel. Observe that the dressing rooms have easy access to both studios and, don't forget, the rehearsal hall. Why tie up a large, expensive studio during off-camera run-thrus?

Note also that the actors avoid the audience area and entrance, and are similarly kept away from the technical operations areas. They further must be "cleared" by the receptionist to get into the "restricted" area.

Equipment moves easily from just about anywhere to the maintenance room. Office and technical personnel may leave the building without having to go through Reception. Vending machines are convenient for actors, office and technical staff.

A film processing room is included for those operations that require it. You may be using reversal film or shoot-and-project negative film.

Often neglected is the announcer's booth. This is where the *offstage voice* makes appropriate "voice-overs" to whatever is appearing on the screen. You could save some money by having *one* announce booth—consisting of video monitor, intercom, announce microphone, and loud-speaker—serve both Studios A and B.

Observe also that the lighting control man has his own isolated booth. In the audience studio he is located in the projection room with the "follow-spot" operator.

A *client's booth* for VIPs is available in the audience studio. The audio and video people are in separate rooms; this has been found to greatly diminish confusion and interference.

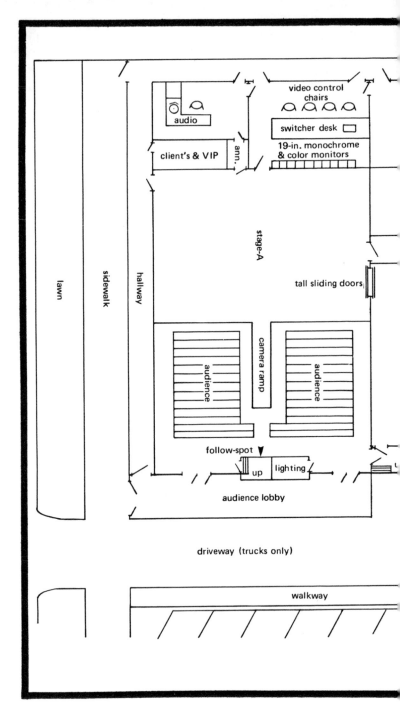

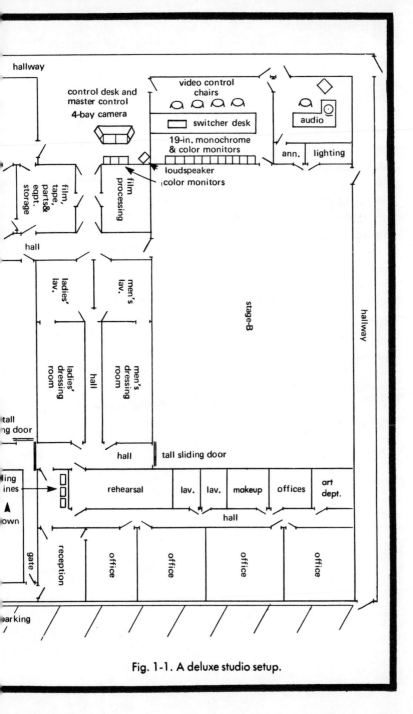

Fig. 1-1. A deluxe studio setup.

11

## Centralized Control

We turn now to the most important of the technical decisions. Instead of locating the camera controls in the studios themselves, control of *all* cameras is centralized in the Master Control Room.

A six-camera array (four live, two film) is barely enough in a two-live-studio installation. By locating all controls in one place, important economies and flexibilities are engendered. First of all, one man can monitor six cameras, whereas splitting the controls could result in requiring as many as three video operators.

Secondly, we can assign up to four cameras to either one of the live studios (the video operator needn't have any interest in the location of the cameras nor the scenes they are shooting).

Finally, we completely unclutter the hectic live studio control rooms by removing the camera controls and their operator. Each video control room has only a monitor for each camera, a video switcher, program and preview monitors and the necessary supplementary facilities.

VTR and Telecine are combined to minimize personnel requirements. Camera Control and Master Control are similarly integrated. Film processing is near the lavatories to reduce plumbing runs, and is near Telecine for fast film handling.

# Chapter 2
## The Multiple Studio—
## Equipment Arrangement
## and Wiring

If you plan to do a significant amount of film editing, your floor plan should include space allocation for a viewing machine and perhaps a projection room. The viewer could be conveniently located either in Telecine or in a portion of the maintenance room (refer to Fig. 1-1 in preceding chapter). Since the Client's Booth in Studio A receives relatively little usage, and since it could offer lounge chairs and other amenities, it makes an excellent projection room. Such facilities, when used for television, normally incorporate a small screen and rear-projection with a projection lamp and screen texture calculated to simulate TV-tube viewing.

You'll observe too that Studio B is so close to the lavatories that it is but a short plumbing run to provide hot and cold water faucets in the studio for the various occasions on which water will be needed. It would also be worthwhile to provide an outlet of natural gas at each soundstage. Don't overlook a drain in each soundstage's floor.

Figure 2-1 details the equipment placement in Master Control. In order to accommodate everything, four racks will be required, possibly more—depending on the physical size of the equipment you purchase. Although control "desks" with sloping turrets are handsome, they are inefficient and impractical. Note that either one or two operators function comfortably, and that racks 1 and 4 are at a convenient angle.

Triangular spacers join all four racks together, and modular assemblies such as these are available from at least three manufacturers. Racks 2 and 3 are shorter than the others, permitting the operator to look over them at the

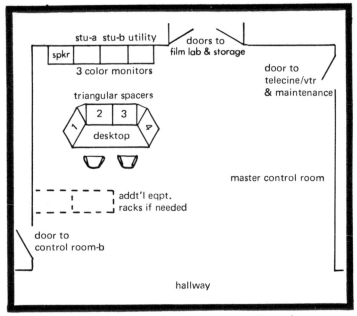

Fig. 2-1. Equipment placement in Master Control.

three 17-in. color monitors suspended from the wall or ceiling. While easy access to the rear of all racks is included, the monitors and high-grade loudspeaker do not require access from the rear. Cable troughs with removable top-plates should be imbedded in the floor in Master Control and in Control Rooms A and B, although overhead cable runs would be more appropriate elsewhere because, for one thing, it is easier to bring cables into the tops of equipment racks than the bottoms, the latter requiring imbedding the cables in troughs in the floor, or raising the racks off the floor.

Figure 2-2 is a block diagram of the video portion of our multistudio layout. A decision had to be made as to whether to choose a patching or routing-switcher interconnect system. The former was chosen because it is cheaper and more compact, and although we have need for considerable circuit routing and rerouting, our setup is not so elaborate that it requires the expense and space of a routing switcher. Patchbays are located in Master Control, Telecine/VTR and Maintenance, and interconnection between these three locations is provided in various ways. We have already decided that there will be no patching in the Studio Control Rooms themselves. Any connections needed to and from the studios are provided for in one or more of the aforementioned three locations.

You will note the extensive use of video distribution amplifiers and there are compelling reason for this. First of all, they prevent any load or any operator error from shorting, interrupting, adding noise to, or in any way disturbing the source. In other words, they are isolation amplifiers. They eliminate imbalances and they permit routing the source to many loads without complicated *loop-thru* systems. Loop-thru is extremely impractical, if not virtually impossible, where patching and signal rerouting is required.

Note also that patching between cameras and camera-control units is provided. This is an inherent part of our versatility and permits us to put up to four cameras in one studio, or three in one and one in the other, or two and two. And, even though the film cameras cannot be moved, placing them in this part of the patching system permits interchange of Camera Control Units in case one fails. We have located the outputs of all camera-cables, and the inputs of all CCUs in rack 4 in Master Control. The connections used here are not jacks but instead are of the type used on the cameras, their cables and their control units, for the interconnecting here involves routing all of the necessary pulses, voltages, and signals associated with each camera.

The diagram in Fig. 2-2 shows what equipment we will be using, how it can or will be interconnected, and approximately where each piece will be physically located. Inasmuch as we have decided to locate as much control as possible in MCR, we would place all possible equipment there, too.

A small but sophisticated video switcher/effects unit will be selected for each of our *two* live studios. It is urgently recommended that such units with *remote* electronics be purchased. The advantages of this are overwhelming. For one thing, you run *no* video cables to the

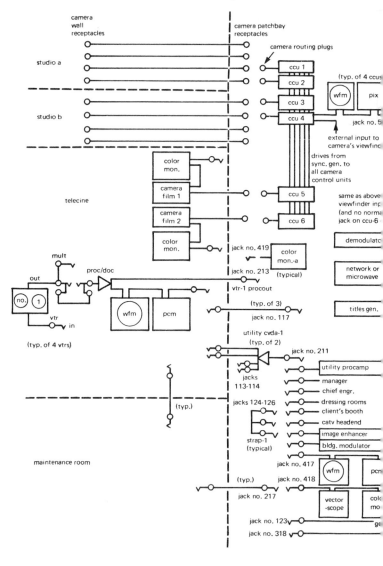

wfm-waveform monitor
pix-monochrome video (picture) monitor
pcm-pulse cross monitor
vtr-video tape recorder

jack numbers shown for reference pertain to Fig. 5-2A, B, C pda-pule distribution isolation amplifier ccu-camera (remote) control unit cvda-composite-video distribution amplifier

camera wall receptacles

camera patchbay receptacles

camera routing plugs

studio a

ccu 1
ccu 2
ccu 3
ccu 4

(typ. of 4 ccus

wfm    pix

jack no. 5

studio b

external input to camera's viewfind

drives from sync. gen. to all camera control units

telecine

color mon.
camera film 1
camera film 2
color mon.

ccu 5
ccu 6

same as above viewfinder inp (and no norma jack on ccu-6

demodulato

jack no. 419

color mon.-a
(typical)

jack no. 213

network or microwave

mult

proc/doc

out

vtr-1 procout

(typ. of 3)
jack no. 117

titles gen.

no. 1

wfm    pcm

vtr in

(typ. of 4 vtrs)

utility cvda-1
(typ. of 2)

jack no. 211

jacks 113-114

utility procamp
manager
chief engr.
dressing rooms
client's booth
catv headend
image enhancer
bldg. modulator

jacks 124-126

(typ.)

strap-1 (typical)

maintenance room

jack no. 417

wfm    pcn

jack no. 418

(typ.)

jack no. 217

vector -scope

colo mo

jack no. 123

ge

jack no. 318

16

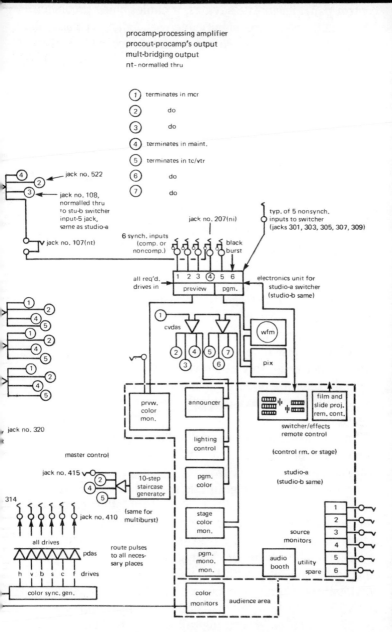

procamp-processing amplifier
procout-procamp's output
mult-bridging output
nt- normalled thru

1 terminates in mcr
2 do
3 do
4 terminates in maint.
5 terminates in tc/vtr
6 do
7 do

jack no. 522

jack no. 108, normalled thru to stu-b switcher input-5 jack, same as studio-a

jack no. 107(nt)

jack no. 207(ni)

typ. of 5 nonsynch. inputs to switcher (jacks 301, 303, 305, 307, 309)

6 synch. inputs (comp. or noncomp.)

black burst

all req'd. drives in

1 2 3 4 5 6
preview   pgm.

electronics unit for studio-a switcher (studio-b same)

cvdas

wfm

pix

prvw. color mon.

announcer

switcher/effects remote control

film and slide proj. rem. cont.

(control rm. or stage)

jack no. 320

lighting control

master control

studio-a (studio-b same)

jack no. 415

10-step staircase generator

pgm. color

jack no. 410

(same for multiburst)

314

stage color mon.

source monitors

all drives

pdas

pgm. mono. mon.

audio booth

utility spare

h v b s c f drives

route pulses to all necessary places

color sync. gen.

color monitors    audience area

Fig. 2-2. Block wiring diagram of Master Control.

17

control panel itself. The savings in cable, noise problems, labor, and space are significant. Secondly, in case of failure, the electronics are much more accessible if they are in Master Control—or even Maintenance. By using the same kind of switchers in both live studios, *one* carefully selected set of spare circuit boards gives superb failure-protection; and of course identical switchers are more convenient for the operators.

One drawback to the array of compact production switchers on the market is that they generally are limited to only six synchronous inputs. Our patching planning permits us to "live with" the situation very nicely, and avoids the expense of larger switcher/effects units. Our patchbay permits MCR to feed each studio *only* the video information it needs for the show it is producing. It further permits changing of sources, if need be, on one or more of the switcher's six inputs during a production.

By the way, don't forget that one input (usually No. 6) of each switcher must be *black*. While it is true that the absence of picture is, in effect, blackness, when "fading to black" you *must* fade to *something, not nothing*. In the latter instance, not only would you lose sync but you would probably see noise and transients on the empty screen. So, we actually use a source of black, which is the *black burst* generator.

In addition to our video distribution amplifiers carrying composite video, designated CVDA, we also use pulse distribution amplifiers (PDA) for all outputs of the sync generator. For one thing, in this manner a sweep circuit failure in any camera will not take all the other cameras along with it down the road to destruction and that could entail many expensive color vidicons or other pickup tubes.

Examination of the block diagram reveals processing amplifiers associated with the VTRs. We have elected to provide three procamps in a four-VTR studio. If necessary, any VTR's output may be patched to any procamp's input (the need for helical processing will be discussed later).

In the case of a VTR and other composite sources, one of its video outputs will be used to feed the *genlock* input of our master sync generator. Genlock is the system that permits roll-free, glitch-free *cuts* (camera outputs are "synchronous" but not necessarily "composite").

An additional processing amplifier is included in MCR to clear up any composite video deemed to be deficient, including adjusting its level. Mixed sync, also designated as sync or "station" sync, may have to be fed into one or more VTRs if they are capable of accepting it.

In order to better understand the patchbays it would help to study the placement of the video equipment in the four racks previously mentioned. Figure 2-3 is our suggestion for operator convenience...either one or two people, depending upon the complexity of the productions in progress. Obviously, exact equipment placement is determined by its size and the user's personal preferences.

Above shelf/desk level we have placed the six CCUs (three each in racks 1 and 4); and in racks 2 and 3 are the six sets of pix (picture) monitor and waveform monitor combinations (a set for each camera). Encoders (NTSC, which also are color-bar generators) are shown with their respective CCUs in case you buy encoders separately from the cameras.

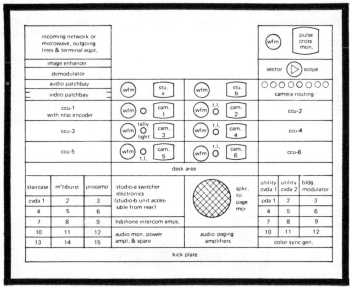

Fig. 2-3. Camera-control operating positions for up to six cameras.

Fig. 2-4. Video jack with BNC connector at rear (above). Gold-plated patching plug for video (below). (Courtesy Trompeter Electronics.)

Video patching (five rows in rack 1) and camera routing (rack 4) are at convenient height when you're standing and the desk portion does not protrude here. Rack 1 also houses a demodulator (TV tuner) and rack 4 a utility waveform and pulse cross pix monitor combination, patchable into any circuit at any time, along with the vectorscope located in rack 4; rack 1 also contains audio patching and incoming microwave or network terminations.

Except where otherwise obvious or noted, all outputs are terminated in 75Ω amplifiers. All other generators, amplifiers and other necessary audio and video equipment are appropriately positioned.

Many people new to studio engineering are unaware of the unique jacks designed to accomplish in video that which we take for granted in audio patching. In video this is more intricate, cumbersome, and expensive, often requiring critical jack location for what is actually a mechanical switching operation effected by insertion of the plug, whereas in audio the switching is essentially electric, permitting widely separated jacks in the same circuit.

Examples of video regular plugs and jacks are shown in Fig. 2-4. Figure 2-5 depicts a loop-thru jack where insertion

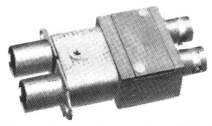

Fig. 2-5. Video twin-jack (vertical mounting) with built-in switching.

of the patchplug into one of the pair breaks the circuit's continuity while plugging to the other does not (bridging).

We will be using all of these in our system. Be sure to use gold-plated video jacks and plugs to assure noise-free high-frequency circuitry. Wiring to video jacks should be to BNC connectors mounted on the rear of the video jacks, rather than via the soldered connections common to audio.

Because of the incredible flexibility of this proposed system "patch planning" is mandatory; otherwise the benefits built-in will never be fully realized. The purpose of our elaborate patchbays, master control, and equipment placement is to (1) permit many things to occur simultaneously, (2) provide some failure protection, and (3) make everybody's job easier and his efforts more successful.

Although camera outputs are, of necessity, synchronous (the horizontal and vertical sweeps are synchronized for "no roll" switching), obtaining H-drive and V-drive pulses from the master sync generator, they may not be composite (video plus sync). Many color cameras offer composite outputs, following the recent broadcast-originated trend, and even low-cost production switchers (Fig. 2-6) often are designed to accept (all) composite or noncomposite sources.

In our proposed system we are going to specify composite camera outputs because, for one thing, with our sync generator genlocked to VTR output (via the VTR's procamp) we could switch from camera to VTR-playback, incorporating fades and effects.

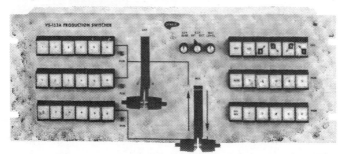

Fig. 2-6. Compact, low-cost professional vertical-interval switcher/ effects unit, remote control section. (Courtesy Dynair Electronics.)

Speaking of *effects*, in color we must be prepared for a phenomenon we are unaccustomed to in monochrome—the effects of *delay*. Because color rendition is determined by the phase angles of the red, green, and blue signals, and because a change of 2 or 3 degrees in the phase information is often enough to cause picture deterioration, and because even minor differences in cable length (or "length" of the circuit routing in the switcher itself) can upset the "delicate color balance," we must make every effort to minimize those differences.

First we must recognize that standard RG-59/U cable has a delay of about 1.4 nanoseconds (about 1.8 degrees) per foot. Secondly, a special-effects generator could introduce to the camera routed to it a delay of as much as 200 nanoseconds.

So, not only should the switcher and effects unit include built-in delay compensation but all sources to the video patchbay (film cameras, live cameras, even VTRs, etc.) should have cables of equal length. Often, sources physically close to the patchbay ay have lengths of RG-59/U cable coiled in an out-of-the-way location so that every cable is the same length. Plug-in delay lines are relatively inexpensive and very compact and accomplish the same purpose. Our patchbay in Master Control provides for insertion, whenever necessary, of delay lines in camera circuits 1 through 5.

The studio control rooms receive and work with that which MCR delegates to them, and the two live studios may be combined to produce a single production if needed.

VTR may be playing to a studio while simultaneously recording a studio's output on another machine, and even transferring film to videotape at the same time or recording an incoming show from network or microwave.

# Chapter 3

# The Single Studio—The Complex Layout

The preceding two chapters on the multiple color studio have, for all intents and purposes, detailed the many structural and circuit requirements of the sophisticated but single-studio facility.

The fact that no control room windows are shown is not an oversight—they are not needed. They are too costly in both labor and materials—especially where soundproofing must be included. Even if they were installed, the view between the studio and its control room would soon be obstructed with sets, drapes, platforms, cameras, people and other equipment. Instead, the cameras are relied upon to let the control room staff see what's going on, to allow the intercom and floor manager to tell the people on stage what to do...and all this can be augmented with two or three judiciously placed small surveillance cameras with wide-angle lenses mounted high on the studio walls and connected to a compact monitor having a selector switch which permits the director or the videoswitcher operator to get any overall view of the studio he desires.

Adjacent to the switcher/effects control panel should be a remote-control unit for the film and slide projectors, essentially identical to their control panel located in Telecine itself. This permits projection (slides and films) to be controlled in the studio that's using it (once it has been set up by the Telecine operator). "Tighter" film integration is the reult, to say nothing of possible savings in manpower (certain film could be preset by the Telecine man who could then move to duties elsewhere, such as VTR operator or in Master Control).

One of the most helpful, yet minor, modifications to existing equipment is the addition of *tally* lights to each monitor associated with a camera. It is extremely inconvenient to depend on the tallylites contained in the pushbuttons of the video switcher, and impossible where camera control is away from camera-switching operations. The camera control operator (shader) should know when a camera is being "taken," as should the *switcher* who does the operation and the director who orders it—to say nothing of the cameramen and performers who watch the tally lights built into the cameras.

In the phonograph record industry it has long been recognized that many of the better audio mixers are artistic folk (often musicians or producers) having only a smattering of technical knowledge. Whereas these people cannot build or repair equipment, they are truly expert in operating it, and achieve superb performances. There is no reason why this should not work in video. This separation of camera control from switcher control allows a technical man to do camera *shading* while a nontechnical man can handle *switching* and *special-effects* creation.

A two-studio operation should entail at least four video tape recorders while an elaborate single studio should have not less than three. Whether for tabletop or floor mounting, VTRs are usually placed along the wall. Associated with each pair of them should be an equipment cabinet containing a waveform monitor and a pulse cross monitor for each VTR. This could be located between each pair of machines. Assuming a four-VTR installation, one of the afore-mentioned cabinets would also contain the Telecine/VTR patchbay. It would also be advisable to include a small color video monitor, with audio, on the output of each film camera, not only to check registration but picture and sound quality as well.

When originally conceived, the video system philosophy called for terminating jacks on virtually all outputs. Since inserting a patchplug into such a jack will break its termination, be certain that each "load" includes a termination of its own to substitute for the one lost during patching. This conception is contrary to that commonly used in audio patching where most loads merely "bridge" a source that is permanently terminated.

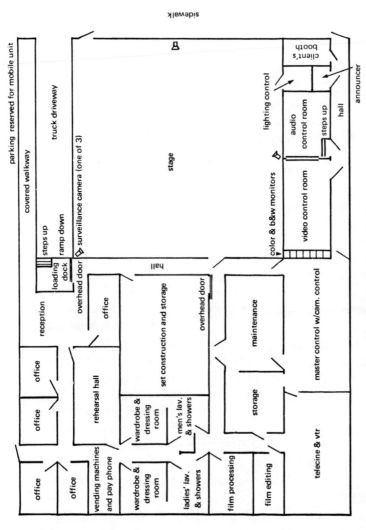

**Fig. 3-1. The complex 1-studio layout.**

25

Inasmuch as the sophisticated single-studio is similar to the multiple studio in purpose, features, and electronics systems design, the foregoing will not be repeated. However, Fig. 3-1 shows a proposed building layout incorporating one large soundstage capable not only of accommodating a number of *standing* sets (which are not dismantled after televising) but also permitting small bleachers to be installed for an audience. Since audiences are planned to be the exception rather than the rule, no provision is made for lobbies, special entrances, or other related facilities. Here the audience is expected to be (more or less) invited guests.

From the floor plan it can be observed that Master Control is out of the way yet centrally located, thus minimizing cable runs. The equipment maintenance room is convenient to every department. The rest rooms, which must include showers for the performers, serve both office and production areas. The plumbing run from rest rooms to film processing, to set construction, and on to the stage is as short as possible (both hot and cold water should be provided at each of these locations).

Vending machines are accessible to all. These are a *must* where people are required to work at night and where costly scheduling must be maintained. A pay telephone should also be located here. (Make sure it is always working!) The rehearsal hall is convenient to both the dressing rooms and the reception—entrance area, where you may wish to station a guard at night to check performers (and crew) in and out. Closed circuit television surveillance might be a substitute when used in conjunction with electrically operated doors.

Note that the soundstage and control rooms are acoustically isolated from other areas wherever possible. The hall provides the special soundproofing between Stage and Set Construction, but between Stage and Truck Driveway soundproofing will be required, and of course between the stage and all control rooms.

Arrange to park the mobile unit, if one is used, near the street so that as many people as possible will see it and learn to recognize it. This can be tremendous free advertising. Place your name and logo on the wall adjacent to the sidewalk.

Whereas it is not our intention to specify dimensions but rather to stress a functional, efficient, and all-encompassing layout, you may wish to consider a soundstage of 40 × 50 ft in a building about 95 ft square overall.

Referring to Fig. 2-3 in the previous chapter will disclose a workable equipment placement in the racks located in the MCR. However, in the case of a single studio, neither the Studio-B monitor nor, probably, camera-4's monitor and CCU (assuming a three-camera array for one studio plus *definitely* two film cameras) would be needed.

A major difference from the floor plan proposed in our sophisticated twin-studio layout earlier in this series is that the audio operator faces the video monitors in the video control room, which he can see through a window dividing the two control rooms. Although not mandatory, this is a common television practice. Being able to see each and all camera outputs instead of merely what's on the program line is often most helpful to the audio mixer.

In most cases it will be necessary to place the audio-control position on a platform a few inches above the video-control floor level so that the audioman can have a better view of the video monitors. Microphone and other cables may be conveniently under this platform. One drawback to this procedure is that all the video monitors must be mounted fairly high on the wall, which means that the video control room people must look *up* at them; this becomes quite a strain after a while.

# Chapter 4

# The Single Studio—The Economy Layout

Prior chapters of this book have covered extensively the elaborate single- and multiple-studio layouts, each an all-encompassing sophisticated production plant capable of the most complex presentations approaching broadcast quality in every respect. Before attaining this goal it may be necessary to make-do with a modicum of equipment.

Unfortunately, people are so inundated with color that they expect nothing less—even in closed-circuit applications; and cable operators face the dilemma of having to place their own programming on the line in competition with slick and expensive Hollywood, New York and European presentations. This situation dictates the need for something more than just a camera, microphone, VTR, and monitor. However, with a little ingenuity the cost can be kept to a minimum.

## Three Is Better Than Two

It might be possible to "squeak through" with two cameras, one of which doubles as both a film and a live vidicon camera (one manufacturer offers a film pedestal which permits the camera to pivot away from the multiplexer to take wide shots of the live action . . . provided it's carefully located). But, it is hoped the system will be able to afford three cameras.

In fact, the versatility and failure protection afforded by three cameras would seem to dictate purchasing three vidicon types rather than two of the superior lead-oxide tube (Plumbicon) units. No attempt will be made here to discuss the differences between single, dual, and triple-tube types. Let it merely be reiterated that you get what you pay for.

Figure 4-1 depicts a block diagram of both the video and the audio systems. Some custom switching has been included in the video circuitry to increase its versatility—primarily by permitting a tape to be aired without tying up the live studio. It is also possible to broadcast a film without it passing through the studio switcher, thus freeing *both* the program *and* the preview buses of the switcher (instead of tying up the program line with the film being aired and thus having only the preview bus left to work with).

Whether your studio is pretentious or spartan, always remember that when switching sources which are nonsynchronous—in this case from switcher to film to VTR, in whatever order—always switch after having faded to (and while in) black. This results in minimum sync disruption to the receivers being fed.

Part of the professionality required of the CCTV system user, and virtually dictated to the CATV operator because of his technical and artistic proximity to the commercial broadcaster, is the use of what is known as a *vertical-interval switcher*.

## Sophistication Plus

This most sophisticated of the three basic switcher design principles accomplishes switches from one input to another during the vertical blanking period, regardless of the moment the switch-button is depressed. Here again the switching takes place during the "black" period. Unless this is done, there will probably be sync disruption to anything on the program line, and this is most damaging to video tape recorders. In fact, most will lose sync on source switching that takes place at other than the vertical interval points.

Fortunately, the development of integrated circuits has dramatically cut the cost of vertical-interval switchers so that now it is possible to purchase a broadcast grade multi-input unit with preview and special effects sections for about a thousand dollars (Fig. 4-2).

There are also some good color synchronizing generators emerging at "livable" prices. Cable operators

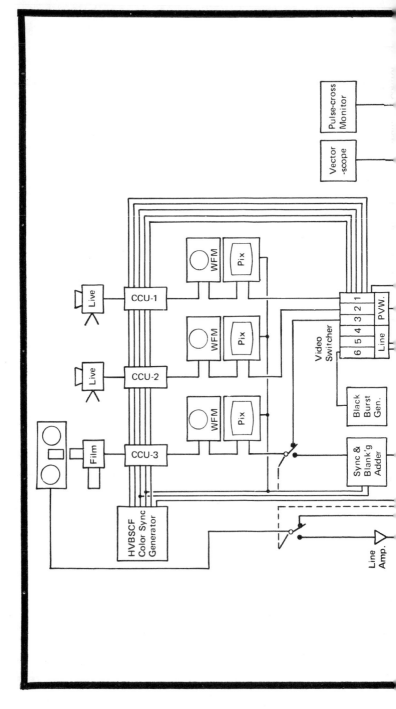

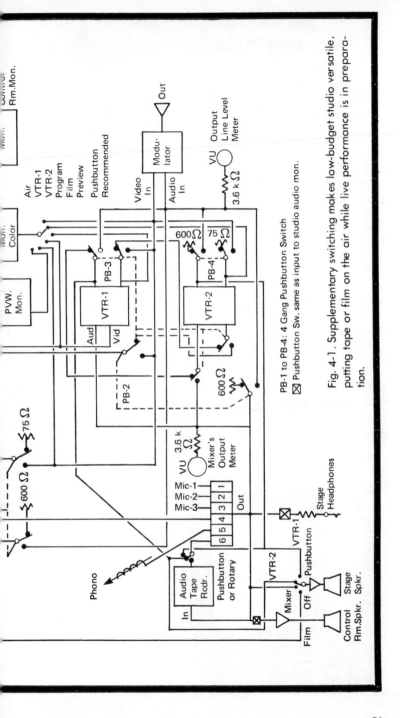

Fig. 4-1. Supplementary switching makes low-budget studio versatile, putting tape or film on the air while live performance is in preparation.

PB-1 to PB-4: 4 Gang Pushbutton Switch

⊠ Pushbutton Sw. same as input to studio audio mon.

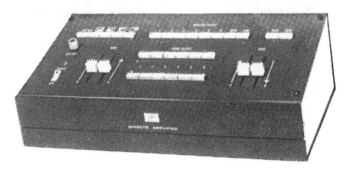

Fig. 4-2. Switcher with special effects. (Courtesy Hitachi-Shibaden.)

should be certain that the generator meets both RS-170 and NTSC specifications; if not, it is not broadcast grade although it may be suitable for most closed-circuit applications. Most lower priced color sync generators do not include genlock or black-burst provisions; the latter should be added to the system and fed to input No. 6 on the switcher to provide a *real black* on picture fade-outs. A pulse cross monitor (Fig. 4-3) not only should be included to read the VTR's playback output in order to optimize tape skew, tracking, and tension but to observe system sync stability in addition to normal picture viewing.

Two VTRs are virtually a *must* for efficient teleproduction in addition to failure security, and one should offer capstan-servo tape editing. If you can afford it, add a helical-scan processing amplifier to clean up the sync

Fig. 4-3. Pulse cross audio—video monitor.

on playback "on the air" or in tape dubbing. Remember that these processors will reshape the sync pulses emanating from the video tape recorder, but will not correct the poor timing stability inherent to all helicals, even though perfect sync was fed in during recording.

Treat yourself to an inexpensive waveform monitor and picture monitor combination (Fig. 4-4) for the outputs of the three cameras. They are truly your best investment as they serve to match the outputs of each camera—all the time—and help to detect interference, sync problems, noise, and even improper scene illumination. By having a waveform monitor on each camera's output, instead of skimping along with only one on the switcher's output, you will be able to monitor sources fed directly to the line without the necessity of running them through the video switcher.

Our audio section permits placing film output or VTR output or mixer output on the line—just as we did in the video section—and avoids mandatory running of everything through the mixer. This frees the mixer for production work while film or tape is on the air. You may wish to tie your audio and video switching together in this area (the popular "audio follows video") to minimize switching effort, especially when operating with skeleton crews.

Figure 4-5 suggests a placement of the equipment in two medium-sized racks. While sloping turrets are attractive and relatively human-engineered, they rarely are able to hold all of the components we must install in a limited space; so they are not recommended.

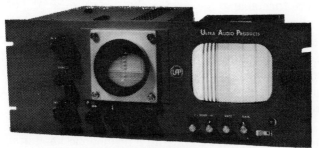

Fig. 4-4. Waveform and video monitor. (Courtesy Ultra Audio Pix-tec.)

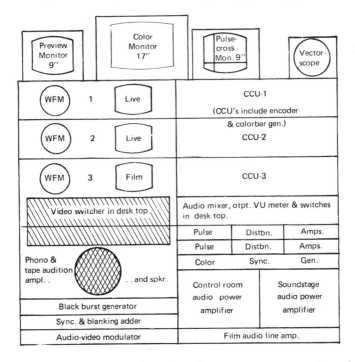

| WFM | 1 | Live | CCU-1 | | |
| | | | (CCU's include encoder | | |
| WFM | 2 | Live | & colorbar gen.) | | |
| | | | CCU-2 | | |
| WFM | 3 | Film | CCU-3 | | |
| Video switcher in desk top | | | Audio mixer, otpt. VU meter & switches in desk top. | | |
| | | | Pulse | Distbn. | Amps. |
| | | | Pulse | Distbn. | Amps. |
| Phono & tape audition ampl.. . . . and spkr. | | | Color | Sync. | Gen. |
| | | | Control room audio power amplifier | Soundstage audio power amplifier | |
| Black burst generator | | | | | |
| Sync. & blanking adder | | | | | |
| Audio-video modulator | | | Film audio line amp. | | |

Fig. 4-5. Desk-top twin racks without sloping turrets accommodate all necessary equipment with some monitors placed on top.

### One or Two Men

The layout described may be conveniently operated by either one or two people. Place all equipment in the room so that the rear of the racks is accessible. You may wish to place one video tape recorder to the operator's left, the disc record turntable to the right of the control desk, the audio tape recorder and second VTR to the operator's rear. Perhaps a remote control for the audio tape recorder could be located at the console for convenience. The Telecine section should be in the normal view of the operator. One color monitor is sufficient for the entire system, although two would be well worthwhile.

Include a utility monochrome monitor for the actors on-stage and provide them with a headphone line for audio (not the intercom) plus a loudspeaker for VTR or film playback. The headphone may be useful for an actor to hear on-the-air audio while he is on the air or to get a cue from the previous program prior to his going on the air.

In closing, a few additional comments relative to the audio – video block diagram are in order. First of all, we have not shown the pulse distribution amplifiers whose absolute essentiality has been previously described. Secondly, we have attempted to overcome the limitations imposed by the lack of elaborate facilities by using ingenious circuitry and supplementary switching.

In most cases here, the use of somewhat more costly and space-consuming pushbutton, rather than rotary, switches will serve to make things easier, speed up production, minimize errors, and preclude the necessity of "scanning" various circuits to get to the desired one.

You may wish to deviate from the VTR routing proposed here, but careful study of the block diagram may persuade you as to the advantages of the proposed setup. Note that the color monitor, vectorscope (if you can afford it) and pulse cross monitor may be bridged onto any circuit, as is the case with the stage monitor for the performers, the latter also are able to hear what's on the line or playback of either VTR.

In the case of PB-1 to PB-4 switchbank, *illuminated* buttons would tell you at a glance what's on the air. Use them in this instance and also in the case of the color monitor. In the latter situation, one of the six pushbuttons is designated "air." During one of the frequent periods of "panic" it is consoling to learn exactly what's on the air at the time without having to stop and think or to look for and study a particular switchbank. (Sometimes you may be horrified to learn that *nothing* is on the air.)

It may also be helpful to have the lights in the buttons of the color monitor source selector switch activated *not* by *their* respective buttons but rather by whatever has been put on the air by the on-the-air selector (PB-1 to PB-4).

Regardless of your budget limitations, if you're a cableman you must remember that *your* originations are competing with television's "best," and you may have to grit your teeth to minimize your disadvantage.

# Chapter 5

# The Color Studio—

# Planning and Construction

Elaborate teleproduction plants may call for the services of an architect or building designer, but whether or not you intend to make use of these specialized skills, the advice of an acoustical consultant may be the most worthwhile investment you can make.

Recording studios present the most serious acoustic problems—very high sound levels that must not penetrate into adjacent studios, so-called *standing waves* of sound, street and other noises that must not be permitted to enter, air-conditioning rumble and "whoosh," rf interference from radio stations, power lines and lighting fixtures, plus the need for decorative interior design.

### Considerations Lessened

These considerations are lessened in the case of soundstages. Here we are working mostly with voice rather than music—although we must be very careful of other noises of all kinds since the voice is not intense enough to drown out radiation interference, street noises, and air-conditioning sounds.

More powerful air conditioning will be required in the color cablecasting studio because of the considerable heat from the lights and the occasionally large number of people that may be on stage, to say nothing of the considerable audio and video equipment in use. Soundstages normally do not devote any attention to decorative walls because they will be covered with drapes, backdrops, and settings for the scenes to be cablecast.

### Expert Helpful

An acoustics expert can detail the construction procedures and materials required to give you the needed soundproofing in only a few hours. This may include construction of walls and ceiling so that no opposite surfaces are parallel. Furthermore, he will more than likely design a "room within a room," with the interior walls completely separate from the exterior walls—an extremely efficient method for sound isolation. He will also specify the methods and special parts required to minimize air-conditioner motor noise and the sound of swirling air.

One of the methods of reducing the cost of soundproofing is the elimination of windows between the studio and the control room. In active cablecasting studios, the windows would normally become useless because of the sets, drapes, personnel, props, and equipment which find their way to this location.

Several manufacturers have introduced ultracompact closed-circuit television surveillance systems of extremely low cost, made possible because up to three cameras may be powered from a single source, and a monitor and camera-switching facility is incorporated into one compact

Fig. 5-1. A monitor which selects up to three surveillance cameras covering the soundstages as an aid to the director and switcher operator. (Courtesy Panasonic.)

cabinet. Not only do these systems cost less than soundproofed windows, but they overcome the problem that occurs when the windows are rendered useless anyway.

## No Fluorescent

In television's early days fluorescent lights were a common occurrence in studios because of their efficiency, minimal heat radiation, and "even" light distribution. Today they should be used only as efficient work lights. So-called down lights, imbedded in the ceiling or suspended from it, should be used in the control room. They should be controlled by an inexpensive dimmer and should be augmented by ample work lights for when the control room equipment is in need of inspection or maintenance.

## Visitor's Window

A window placed between the control room and the hallway is highly recommended. Visitors may then watch the always interesting control room activity without entering the room (you could use curtains or venetian blinds to prevent this when desired) and staff members in search of someone could see whether or not that person is in the control room without having to enter and disturb its occupants.

In an elaborate plant desiring the utmost in versatility and flexibility at the lowest possible cost, all important areas should be interconnected via appropriate patchbays, both audio and video. These would include at least two or three "open loops" from location to location—such as Master Control to each studio Control Room, Master Control to Telecine/VTR, Master Control to Maintenance, and Telecine/VTR to Maintenance. These lines terminate in jacks so that "information" may be sent in either direction. The ultimate convenience and "fail-safe" aspects of these provisions more than justify their relatively modest cost.

Figure 5-2 details an extensive patchbay intended originally for use in the sophisticated two-studio setup described in an earlier chapter. As has been pointed out before, the physical placement of video jacks is far more critical than is the case with audio jacks. This results from "looping and loading" conditions inherent to video which require certain jacks to be adjacent (usually vertically).

Careful study of the patchbays will reveal that concerted attention has been given to obtaining a logical, efficient, and functional placement of all video jacks. The bays shown here make use of specially designed video jacks, not found (nor necessary) in audio. The many multiple outputs used for certain circuits are necessary to feed some of the outputs to various points simultaneously.

It is customary in cablecasting studios to minimize construction costs by running cables overhead and more or less exposed, as opposed to the concealed wiring common in radio stations and recording studios. Entry to the equipment racks is made at the top, rather than through conduit or ducting installed at the base of the racks. While video cable runs are not very attractive, their utility and cost savings should be a prime consideration.

Multiconductor camera cables, control wires, video lines, audio lines, and in certain instances, lighting cables, may be supported by *cable trays* which are suspended from the walls or ceiling. Special sections for all sorts of sizes and styles of trays are available to provide sharp or gentle bends in the cable being supported, inside or outside slopes . . *everything* necessary to direct the cables properly with a minimum of strain plus the all-important accessibility and the ability to remove or add wires easily. Figure 5-3 depicts these cable-carrying units.

While video cables generally carry about equal voltages, this is not the case with audio. Care should be taken to keep microphone cables (usually at −56 dB level) away from program lines which are at +4 or +8 dB. Failure to do so could mean pickup of program material in the microphone lines. Of course, *everything* should be kept away from ac power cables and lighting wiring. Separate entrances to the racks for each type of "service" should be provided.

There is a great danger of leakage and interference when wires parallel each other for any appreciable distance. While your ac power to the racks will probably

NT—Normalled Through jack to jack directly below
NI—Normalled Input
T—Output jack with built-in 75 ohm terminating resistor

I—Input
F—Feed to or from another location
S—Strapping circuit
X—spare

WFM—Waveform Monitor
PCM—Pulse Cross Monitor
V-Scope—Vectorscope
VDA—Video Distribution Amplifier
CVDA—Composite-Video Distribution Amplifier

PDA—Pulse Distribution Amplifier
M—"Mult" Bridging Output
B—Bridging Input

**ROW 1**

| NT | NT | NT | NT | NT | NT | NT | NT | T |
|----|----|----|----|----|----|----|----|---|
| 101 | | | 104 | | | 107 | | |
| CAMERA NO 1 | CAMERA NO 1 | CAMERA NO 2 | CAMERA NO 2 | CAMERA NO 3 | CAMERA NO 3 | CAMERA NO 4 | CAMERA NO 4 | FILM CAM 1 |

**ROW 2**

| NI | NI | NI | NI | NI | NI | NI | NI | NI |
|----|----|----|----|----|----|----|----|----|
| 202 | | | 205 | | | 208 | | |
| CONTROL ROOM-A IN-1 | CONTROL ROOM-B IN-1 | CONTROL ROOM-A IN-2 | CONTROL ROOM-B IN-2 | CONTROL ROOM-A IN-3 | CONTROL ROOM-B IN-3 | CONTROL ROOM-A IN-4 | CONTROL ROOM-B IN-4 | CONTROL ROOM-A IN-5 |

**ROW 3**

| I | I | I | I | I | I | I | I | I |
|---|---|---|---|---|---|---|---|---|
| 303 | | | 306 | | | 309 | | |
| STUDIO-A NON-SYNC IN 1 | STUDIO-B NON-SYNC IN 1 | STUDIO-A NON-SYNC IN 2 | STUDIO-B NON-SYNC IN 2 | STUDIO-A NON-SYNC IN 3 | STUDIO-B NON-SYNC IN 3 | STUDIO-A NON-SYNC IN 4 | STUDIO-B NON-SYNC IN 4 | STUDIO-A NON-SYNC IN 5 |

**ROW 4**

| T | T | T | T | T | T | T | T | T |
|---|---|---|---|---|---|---|---|---|
| 401 | | | 404 | | | 407 | | |
| STUDIO-A OUT | STUDIO-A OUT | STUDIO-A OUT | STUDIO-B OUT | STUDIO-B OUT | STUDIO-B OUT | MIXED SYNC | MIXED SYNC | MXD BLNK'G |

**ROW 5**

| I | I | I | I | I | I | X | X | I |
|---|---|---|---|---|---|---|---|---|
| 502 | | | 505 | | | 508 | | |
| STU-A MON-1 | STU-A MON-2 | STU-A MON-3 | STU-A iMON-4 | STU-A MON-5 | STU-A MON-6 | SPARE | SPARE | STU-B MON-1 |

**Fig. 5-2A. Patchbay dedication for Master Control.**

**Row 100 (111–126)**

| Port | Type | Designation |
|---|---|---|
| 111 | T | FILM CAM 2 |
| 112 | T | FILM CAM 2 |
| 113 | T | VTR CVDA-1 OUTPUT |
| 114 | T | VTR CVDA-1 OUTPUT |
| 115 | T | VTR CVDA-2 OUTPUT |
| 116 | T | VTR CVDA-2 OUTPUT |
| 117 | F | TC/VTR-1 |
| 118 | F | TC/VTR-2 |
| 119 | F | TC/VTR 3 |
| 120 | I | BUILDING MODULATOR |
| 121 | T | HORIZONTAL DRIVE |
| 122 | T | VERTICAL DRIVE |
| 123 | I | GENLOCK IN |
| 124 | S | STRAP-1 |
| 125 | S | STRAP-1 |
| 126 | S | STRAP-1 |

**Row 200 (211–226)**

| Port | Type | Designation |
|---|---|---|
| 211 | I | VTR CVDA-1 IN |
| 212 | I | VTR CVDA-2 IN |
| 213 | T | VTR-1 PROC OUT |
| 214 | T | VTR-2 PROC OUT |
| 215 | T | VTR-3 PROC OUT |
| 216 | T | VTR-4 PROC OUT |
| 217 | F | MAINTENANCE-1 |
| 218 | F | MAINTENANCE-2 |
| 219 | T | DEMODULATOR |
| 220 | T | DEMODULATOR |
| 221 | F | CHIEF ENGR |
| 222 | F | GEN'L MGR. |
| 223 | I | CLIENT'S BOOTH |
| 224 | S | STRAP-2 |
| 225 | S | STRAP-2 |
| 226 | S | STRAP-2 |

**Row 300 (311–326)**

| Port | Type | Designation |
|---|---|---|
| 311 | T | TITLES GEN OUT |
| 312 | T | TITLES GEN OUT |
| 313 | I | IMAGE ENHANCER IN |
| 314 | T | IMAGE ENHANCER OUT |
| 315 | T | STUDIO-A PREVIEW OUT |
| 316 | T | STUDIO-B PREVIEW OUT |
| 317 | I | DRESSING ROOMS |
| 318 | I | STUDIO-A AUDIENCE MON. |
| 319 | I | PROCAMP (UTILITY) IN |
| 320 | T | PROCAMP OUT |
| 321 | T | PROCAMP OUT |
| 322 | I | CATV HEADEND IN |
| 323 | I | CAMERA-1 VIEWFINDER IN |
| 324 | I | CAMERA-2 VIEWFINDER IN |
| 325 | I | CAMERA-3 VIEWFINDER IN |
| 326 | I | CAMERA-4 VIEWFINDER IN |

**Row 400 (411–426)**

| Port | Type | Designation |
|---|---|---|
| 411 | T | BLACK BURST |
| 412 | T | COLOR BURST |
| 413 | T | MULTIBURST |
| 414 | T | MULTIBURST |
| 415 | T | STAIRCASE |
| 416 | T | STAIRCASE |
| 417 | I | UTILITY WFM & PCM |
| 418 | I | UTIL. COLOR MON & V-SCOPE |
| 419 | I | COLOR MON. A |
| 420 | I | COLOR MON. |
| 421 | T | NETWORK OR MICROWAVE |
| 422 | T | |
| 423 | S | STRAP-4 |
| 424 | S | STRAP-4 |
| 425 | S | STRAP-4 |
| 426 | S | STRAP-4 |

**Row 500 (511–526)**

| Port | Type | Designation |
|---|---|---|
| 511 | I | STU-B MON-3 |
| 512 | I | STU-B MON-4 |
| 513 | I | STU-B MON-5 |
| 514 | I | STU-B MON-6 |
| 515 | T | CAM-1 OUT |
| 516 | T | CAM-1 OUT |
| 517 | T | CAM-2 OUT |
| 518 | T | CAM-2 OUT |
| 519 | T | CAM-3 OUT |
| 520 | T | CAM-3 OUT |
| 521 | T | CAM-4 OUT |
| 522 | T | CAM-4 OUT |
| 523 | T | CAM-5 OUT |
| 524 | T | CAM-5 OUT |
| 525 | T | CAM-6 OUT |
| 526 | T | CAM-6 OUT |

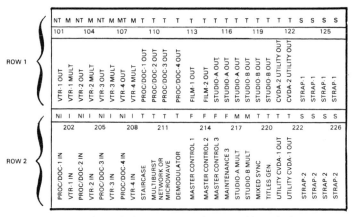

Fig. 5-2B. Telecine/videotape recording patchbay dedication.

Fig. 5-2C. Maintenance dept. patchbay dedication.

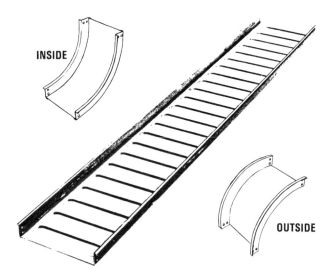

Fig. 5-3. Straight cable tray and two types of vertical bends. (Courtesy Chalfant Products Co.)

have to be encased in approved conduit, it is sometimes possible to run wiring to your stage-set lights without having to use conduit. Usually, the way to do so is to have all such wires utilize plugs at the "cold" end and use cable that is rubber-covered and not fastened anywhere—so that it is legally "portable" according to the electrical code definition. Your cable trays help make this possible, and the cost saving is fantastic.

# Chapter 6

## The Complete Picture—Laying It on the Line

How do you know how good your picture is? Will your picture be of the same quality tomorrow as it is today? Will one technician or one group of technical crewmen give you the same technically correct pictures as another? The cable operator who must compete with "Hollywood's Best," and the CCTV industrial-educational studio which must deliver attention-getting (and holding) videotapes, are expected to present pictures of technical quality substantially on a par with those produced by the broadcast-grade production houses. More than your cameras and switcher/effects equipment, your *support equipment* make this possible.

Except for what might be called "tabletop systems" (consisting of only a camera, microphone, video tape recorder, and a monitor), even the most modest of production plants must have a device that generates synchronizing pulses, commonly known as a sync generator. With the use of integrated circuits becoming commonplace, even a color sync generator of broadcast quality becomes relatively modest in cost. The color sync generator incorporates all the features of a monochrome unit plus two additional outputs—burst flag and color subcarrier.

Without getting too technical, let us examine the functions of the sync generator. The *horizontal* and the *vertical drive* outputs are designed primarily to synchronize the *sweep* circuits in all your cameras. Without this there would be picture disturbances each time you switch from one camera to another. Cameras will generate their own sync pulses internally, unless designed to receive sync from an external source. The H-drive pulses from the sync generator lock the horizontal (left-to-right) traces of the scanning beam of the pickup tubes so that all cameras sweep together. The V-drive pulses return the electron beams from the end of their sweep at the lower right corner to the beginning of the next sweep at the top left.

The composite blanking pulses from the sync generator serve to darken the horizontal traces as the electron beam returns from tracing a scan line to begin the next line. Similarly. the vertical blanking pulses provide a longer interval of darkness (about 20 or 21 lines worth) to allow the beam to return in darkness from the bottom to the opposite corner at the top.

Interestingly, the vertical retrace is not direct. The beam actually bounces from side to side a few times before arriving at its starting point. You can often observe this by increasing the brightness control setting on your video monitor to the point of overcoming the blanking effect. Certain cameras generate their own blanking internally and do not require external blanking pulses.

The *composite sync* (often called *mixed sync*) *output* includes the two drive pulses plus equalizing pulses necessary to maintain sync to FCC tolerances. These latter signals may easily be seen on a pulse cross monitor. Broadcast sync specifications are extremely stringent (probably more so than for the pictures themselves) because millions of television receivers must lock (synchronize) to these pulses (or suffer picture "tearing" and "roll"). The four aforementioned outputs are "negative going" to eliminate interaction with the picture information, and are provided by the sync generator at an amplitude of 4V each.

Figure 6-1 shows their shape and timing and also includes a comparison with the European CCIR monochrome standards. The sync pulses also make possible the interlace of odd- and even-numbered scal lines, 26½ of each, so that a complete picture of the highest possible vertical resolution is obtained.

Two additional pulses are created by the color-sync generator, the most important of these being the color (reference) burst. This 3.57954 MHz (3.58) pulse, which is held to a duration of eight to eleven cycles, appears at the

## Waveform

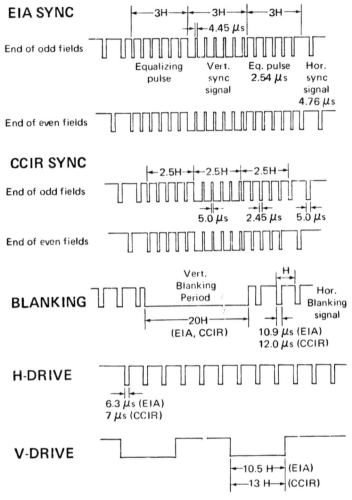

Fig. 6-1. The four primary pulses of the sync generator, including a comparison with European monochrome standards.

beginning of each horizontal line. The color burst has no color in it per se; instead it is used by each camera's color encoder to compare against the "nonstandard" colors being picked up by the camera tubes.

Since the color encoder generates only some six basic colors (plus white—all colors, and black—no colors) it must have something to compare the other-than-basic colors with. The color burst is the comparison reference and permits the changes in phase of the signals that give us the many different hues.

Finally, we encounter what is known as the *burst flag*. This pulse is coincident with the color reference burst and thus appears on what is called *back porch* of the horizontal blanking area (the section just prior to blanking is known as the *front porch*). Its purpose is to gate-in the color burst information. Many color cameras designed to American television standards do not require burst flag from the sync generator because the cameras generate their own gating pulses.

You will most likely want to purchase a sync generator incorporating the "genlock" provision allowing you to synchronize your entire video system to an external video source (VTR, remote line, etc.) when needed—a worthwhile additional expenditure. This is the only *input* on your sync generator, and it accepts a composite (pix plus mixed sync) video signal, although it discards the video information. The term "phase lock" is substituted for "genlock" in color work because the "genlock" is to the phase of the incoming color reference burst.

Figure 6-2 shows the basic colors (EIA spec RS-189) generated by each camera's encoder. They may be displayed on a TV monitor and are useful for setting hue and saturation (color intensity) prior to going on the air. This should be done on all color monitors, matching them as closely as possible. Because colors are subjective, other devices may be required so that your color is uniform throughout the broadcast day and from day to day.

This brings us to one of the most crucial matters, that which is often referred to as "setup." You have made a costly investment in cameras, switchers, special effects, image enhancers, chroma key, luminance/chrominance normalizers, aperture correction, and many other useful devices. But are you ready to go "on the air?" The answer is a positive *no*. Because first you must check your system's quality and to do that you must first "calibrate" your monitors. So, in addition to the aforementioned color bars

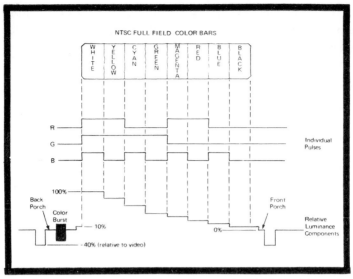

Fig. 6-2. The green, red, and blue pulses create 8 individual hues; the relative intensity of each is also shown.

you will need two other important generators—staircase and multiburst.

Camera color encoders normally offer only what are know as *full* bars. These are as shown in Fig. 6-2. But there are also *split bars* which put the white and the black bursts below the group of six basic colors, instead of adjacent to them; and there is the new *split field*—seven shades of neutral grays, rather than just white and black, located below all the bars depicted in Fig. 6-2.

The value of the latter is that they are able to clearly disclose the effects of luminance/chrominance time delay. If you do not care to purchase a split-field color-bar generator you must acquire a staircase generator. These create ten steps of gray beginning with black and ending with white. They are created in such a way that the intensity of each step is 10% different from that of the adjacent steps. The signals from the "step" generator are shown on a waveform monitor in Fig. 6-3A and on a video monitor in Fig. 6-3B.

Because they run the gamut of lighting intensities that you will encounter in the scenes you televise, the

Fig. 6-3A. Staircase pattern as shown on waveform monitor. (Courtesy Ultra Audio Pixtec.)

Fig. 6-3B. Ten-step shown on pulse cross monitor in normal display mode. (Courtesy Ultra Audio Pixtec.)

staircase signal is ideal for setting contrast and brightness on all your monitors. Set brightness first, by ascertaining that you have the best possible black, while the nine other shades are discernible. Then set contrast so that the white bar is as bright as possible without "blooming." Your monitors will then be properly calibrated for luminance.

"Step" is also excellent for setting the gain on your video tape recorder—although some inexpensive VTRs may require color bars rather than staircase because they will not accept as much luminance in the color mode as when they are recording monochrome. Because of this, picture distortions of many types would take place.

The waveform monitor (WFM) is your best friend in the studio. It is an extremely reliable tool that will tell you

Fig. 6-4A. Multiburst display in waveform monitor. (Courtesy Ultra Audio Pixtec.)

Fig. 6-4B. Multiburst signal gives quick check on studio bandwidth by showing where black and white areas merge. (Courtesy Ultra Audio Pixtec.)

many things that the cheap video-level meters either do not disclose or disclose inaccurately. Meters such as those on some cameras and video tape recorders are averaging devices. They are slow acting, read rms instead of p-p (peak-to-peak) video levels, indicate lower than correct intensities, and do not show the intensities of the many different portions of the scene being televised.

The WFM overcomes this unreliability, and you should have one on each camera's output. This is made possible by recently introduced low-cost waveform monitors. Referring to Fig. 6-3, you will see the various intensities of the step pattern just as though a camera were photographing a card having ten shades of gray. The scene is displayed twice so that you can see the horizontal blanking in the sync area (below the "zero" line) between two video lines.

Observe that the WFM tells you the intensity of every individual portion of the entire scene, from left to right. It will also indicate differences in brightness from top to bottom of the scene, as would be evidenced by a bunching-up of the WFM's scan lines making them appear to be brighter portions of the scene.

The second of our two important pieces of setup equipment is known as *multiburst*. Figure 6-4 shows a burst pattern as would be seen on a waveform monitor and on a video monitor. Multiburst means exactly what it says—a series of short bursts at various, increasing frequencies, preceded by a "white flag" area. The frequencies normally used are 0.5, 1.25, 2.0, 3.0, 3.58, and 4.1 MHz. By using multiburst you can make a quick and reliable test of the frequency response (bandwidth) of your studio facilities (and an entire CATV system as well). Using a monitor of known high resolution (8 MHz is recommended) you can place it anywhere in your video lines to see how good the frequency response of that portion of the system is.

At the burst where you cannot differentiate between the black and white lines you will determine the bandwidth of your system. For example, if you cannot see black and white distinct lines on the 4.1 MHz burst, your bandwidth would be less than this. In this respect, note the slight taper in height of the higher frequency bursts as shown on the WFM in Fig. 6-4, indicating that frequency response of the system being measured began to drop off a little above the 2 MHz point.

Now that your waveform monitors have aided you in establishing proper video levels—and even proper scene lighting, your picture monitors have been calibrated with staircase signals, the chrominance has been adjusted with color bars, and your frequency response has been confirmed with multiburst, you are ready to begin the day's transmissions or videotaping. There are, of course, various other, sometimes more sophisticated, tests, such as for hum and low-frequency distortions ("tilt"), ringing, sync stability, luminance/chrominance abnormalities, etc.; but these need not be made daily.

# Chapter 7
# Putting the Good
# Ideas to Work

In previous chapters, we have discussed aspect of design, construction, equipment selection, operation, and maintenance of low-cost color television production facilities—from modest budget-conscious layouts to more pretentious all-encompassing schemes. We have observed that "low cost" is only relative (in comparison to commercial television studios), and that color per se is costly. Along the way, you may have wondered whether some of the writer's recommendations were "theoretical" and not truly practical.

Well, in three parts, we will describe an *actual studio* we built which incorporates as many of the previously espoused principles as could possibly be applied. If any have been omitted or "contradicted," it is due solely to the budget and physical limitations dictated by the conditions under which we had to operate. For the first and only time in these chapters, we will specify the brand of equipment we chose and, where appropriate, why it was selected. Although we will present no cost breakdown, the total value of the equipment in use is $ 200,000. While this constitutes a formidable investment, bear in mind that it equals the cost of just *one* of the best broadcast color cameras coupled with one high-band quadruplex video tape recorder.

### Philosophy and Floor Plan

The reader should be reminded that the primary criterion was to create a studio capable of being dismantled and loaded on a truck. Telecine equipment was excluded, but the array does include a quadruplex video tape recorder (oh yes, we master on quadruplex). Furthermore, the transformation must be done in less than one hour's time and using only two people (which we've done many times).

At Telaudio, the author's studio, we feel that unless a user has constant need of remote operations, the worst thing he can do is build a permanent remote van. The reasons for this are numerous: well designed air-conditioned vans are expensive; equipment is exposed to undue risk of theft and damage; quarters are cramped to work in; access to equipment for maintenance purposes is a real headache; grounding problems occur; rarely does space permit inclusion of everything you need—to say nothing of the virtual impossibility of temporary additions or changes that always seem to crop up.

So, get the stars out of your eyes and forget the glamorous remote truck—rent yourself a van with an electric tailgate whenever you go on "remotes." And, when you do, remember our previous warnings that remoted locations rarely offer enough ac power from a single outlet to run all of your color equipment, not to mention any lights you may require. So plan to operate from within a building at the remote site rather than run long power lines (with intolerable voltage drop) to your mobile control room. This way you not only avoid the very expensive long color-camera cables and the personnel needed to pull them, but also the visitors who are likely to damage them.

We were not afforded the luxury of being able to design our studio from the ground up. Instead, we had to fit it into a rather small area. Figure 7-1 is a floor plan in which you will note that we've not overlooked the all-important dressing rooms and storage areas. Note also that the lavatory is accessible to both actors and crew, and that actors need not pass through the soundstage to get to it from the dressing rooms. Please bear in mind that the lavatory was already a fixed location and that water occasionally needed onstage must come from there. For what it is worth, the front door was also a fixed point that we had to contend with.

In spite of minimal square footage, we made a decision that we have never regretted—we sacrificed some stage size to afford ourselves a relatively spacious control room. After all, the critical and nerve-wracking work is done

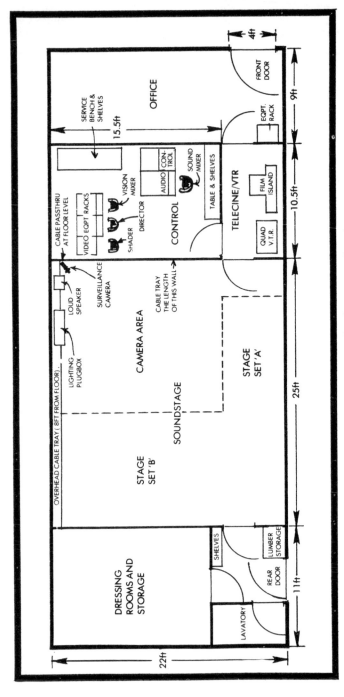

Fig. 7-1. Floor plan of a modest but practical studio.

there. Everything possible should be done to make it comfortable and convenient at all times. And rest assured, there will always be unexpected VIPs and equipment problems. We found it expedient to locate the equipment maintenance workbench in our control room, although we would have preferred a separate room. (We'd have *preferred* many different things, but we've learned to *make do* with many invariably unavoidable restrictions, just as you will have to do, no doubt.)

As can be seen from the floor plan, the soundstage is rather small. When our clients require a larger stage, we move our entire video array—cameras, racks, VTR, and all—to a motion-picture soundstage available at fairly reasonable rental rates. Surprisingly, we not only create rather lavish productions within our confined quarters, but we even have two distinct "acting areas"—one about twice the size of the other.

### Quality of Equipment

Decisions with respect to the overall quality of the equipment are always hard to make. In video, as in so many areas, the more you spend the better the equipment is. After considerable evaluation and soul-searching, we decided to create a studio built around "bottom-of-the-line" broadcast-grade equipment. This dictated lead-oxide three-tube cameras; two *used* low-band quadruplex VTRs with electronic editing; dim and nondim lighting circuits; self-contained telecine/VTR equipment that can function independently when the production control-room is being used for other purposes or is on a truck "on location" somewhere; and finally some very elaborate audio capabilities normally overlooked by inexperienced studio designers who lack control room operating experience. These fellows always end up adding a modicum of audio as an "afterthought"—very likely they don't have the understanding of audio to do a competent job of custom designing in the first place.

Figure 7-2 shows the camera area as seen from "Set B" where we're getting ready to shoot some tabletop products on "Set A," shown in Fig. 7-3. Although more are available,

Fig. 7-2. Chief camerman doubles as lighting director in a small TV studio equipped to do broadcast-grade production. (Courtesy Telaudio Centre. Photo by Don Lauritzen.)

we are regularly rigged for five focusing 1000W scoops with color frames and 12 500W Fresnels, some on pantographs with colorframes and four-way barn doors, plus one "Lekolite" ellipsoidal 500W spotlight normally used as a pattern projector. The primary 100A power service consists of 50A on a Century-Strand "Dimmy" two-scene preset dimmer bank, whose compact remote-control unit is operated on stage during setup, then from the control room during production. All luminaires are Century and all lamps are either 3000 or 3200° Kelvin color temperature. Any light may be directly plugged into any dim, or any one of six nondim circuits for which the remaining 50A are used without the need for patch panels. This approach keeps our lighting equipment flexible, yet with the least possible investment.

Sets "A" and "B" are carpeted while the camera area has linoleum. The cameras are Hitachi Shibaden with industrial-grade Plumbicon tubes. We do not use extended-red tubes because these cameras are equipped with both red-stimulator circuits and a 6 dB boost provision when needed. ITE pan-tilt heads support each camera and

Fig. 7-3. Lady cameraperson lends art director and author (right) a hand in setting up cosmetics commercial in small stage. (Courtesy Telaudio Centre. Photo by Don Lauritzen.)

its 10:1 zoom lens. We have a loudspeaker on-stage for talkback and playback to the actors and crew, plus a large Conrac monochrome monitor and a World Video portable color monitor. These are used for both videotape playback and for cueing the actors. A background is either Set "A" or "B." Drapes also serve to reduce reverberation. A connector box accepting up to six microphones may be placed wherever convenient, and the cameras may be pointed at either set at any time during production, often without changing their positions.

Finally, a small Panasonic surveillance camera with a wide-angle lens is used for overall views of the soundstage from the control room, eliminating the need for costly and superfluous control-room windows. Placed high, the camera allows the director, audioman, and vision mixer to check the location of personnel and properties that may not be picked up by the production cameras and might be hidden from view through a window by cameras, personnel, sets props, backgrounds, drapes, and lights. Contrary to motion picture and theatre lighting, in television we try never to operate any set-lighting equipment on the floor.

Next we will describe in detail the control-room facilities; after that—Telecine and VTR operations.

# Chapter 8

# The Arrangement of Equipment Pays

Previously we discussed the floor plan of the entire studio complex with special attention to the soundstage and the equipment on it. Now we cover the nerve center—the control room. The reader is again asked to bear in mind that the equipment selected is that deemed most appropriate to our budget and quality criteria, and the layout and placement was dictated by the requirement that all equipment (except for lights and telecine) be capable of being dismantled and loaded onto a truck within an hour's time for location shooting.

## AUDIO CONTROL

Observe in Fig. 8-1 that, as in all broadcast-grade installations, and contrary to most industrial and other low-budget studios, audio is located separately from video. In our case, audio (photo, far right) is housed in two separate desk consoles, Fig. 8-2. The left-hand unit contains amplifiers, switching and control; the right-hand unit contains a professional remote-controlled 7.5 – 15 ips Revox two-channel $\frac{1}{4}$ in. audio tape recorder equipped with "sel-sync" for overdubbing and variable speed, plus a Panasonic disc turntable (installed in the desk portion of the console). Both consoles are on casters for mobility, but if the tape and disc isn't needed on a "remote" it stays in the control room. Both the disc and tape may be operated without the mixing console when that console is away. This is possible because we amplify the disc pickup to zero-level via an inexpensive Ramko amplifier.

Going from bottom to top, the audio-control console contains a number of units. In the base, facing the audioman's knees, is the audition-cue loudspeaker. Behind

Fig. 8-1. Broadcaster-style control room separates audio (right) from video. Service bench is handy at rear. (Courtesy Telaudio Centre. Photo by Don Lauritzen.)

it, and accessible from the rear, are the three power amplifiers, Jerrold solid-state units of 35W capability. One amplifier is for stage paging (by director, vision mixer, or audioman) and audio playback (audio tape, videotape, film) or audio-mixer monitoring. The third amplifier is for control-room monitoring of anything.

In the control area of the console, we have a five-input mixer for our Sennheiser microphones with master gain control and VU meter, a custom-built unit by Ultra Audio

Fig. 8-2. Flexible and elaborate high-level and low-level audio array is in two separate consoles for convenience. Note unique method of installing turntable in desk area. (Courtesy Telaudio Centre. Photo by Don Lauritzen.).

Products, incorporating straight-line gain controls. Above it are a pair of Ultra Audio 9 in. monochrome pulse cross monitors, permitting the audioman to watch anything he desires for convenience, usually PREVIEW and PROGRAM. He needs these because he often can't see the director's monitors. Upon request, he can place the monitors in pulse-cross mode to check sync stability of program or tape playback if desired by the vision mixer. Directly above these monitors is the heart of audio control—a custom-built Ultra Audio setup switchpanel.

The switchpanel contains three eight-button rows of rear-illuminated Switchcraft push-switches. Each bank feeds the appropriate power-amplifier previously described. The same eight sources are fed to all three switchbanks, permitting any monitor amplifier to take any of the eight sources while the other monitor amplifiers may simultaneously take the same or any of the other sources. This extreme flexibility is usually found only in customized professional audio. It is a *must*—an arrangement means live sound can be heard and recorded and played back for actors and/or the director. It means film-sound can be auditioned; discs cued; audio tape played, mixed, or cued. It means even other sources of audio can be connected, mixed, and checked. The eight pushbuttons in each of the three banks are engraved as follows and are illuminated only when depressed: FILM. VTR 1. VTR 2. ATR 1. ATR 2. AUX 1. AUX 2. MIXER.

Adjacent to each switchbank is its volume control, plus a gain control for the phono cue circuit. Inset in the panel is a paging microphone, its on-off switch and volume control. Finally, there are three gain controls for high-level/low-impedance patch-in sources and two for high-level/high-impedance sources. A very handy built-in tone generator makes possible quick synchronizing of all VU meters in the system. Above this panel is the patchbay which permits, among other things, connecting any high-level source to any mixing control. Note that any source may be switched to any power amplifier (driving an Acoustic Research monitor speaker) for any listening purpose without having to first patch it to a mixer pot. The microphone mixer contains the overall audio grand master. All microphone lines are plugged directly into the back of the mixer while all high-level sources in and out of the console connect to "XL" plugs at console-rear where the power-amp controls are. Emergency connections, however, may be made directly to the patchbay.

A UAP "outboard" mixer, connectable via "XL" plug or patchcord, gives us five more microphone inputs. Following good audio practice, the Switchcraft patchbay provides both terminating and bridging ("mults") outputs for each source, so that they may be properly connected and heard. Three groups of "strap" jacks are provided, so that various distinct sources may be connected to more than one load. These straps also permit intermixing of old-style (but still popular) twin-plugs with the more compact tip-ring-sleeve plugs. This convenience is often necessary when connecting to other people's equipment.

Finally, we have made provision to accept and/or feed industrial-grade VTRs that offer hi-Z and/or unbalanced lo-Z circuitry. This is done in two ways. We built compact interface-boxes containing transformers to convert the "amateur" VTRs to professional circuit standards. We also provide hi-Z inputs and outputs on our consoles. Because the audio output of a "tabletop" VTR is usually 0.1V, 500$\Omega$ unbalanced our interface permits step-up to higher level via a high-turns-ratio Triad transformer; and, for even more gain, we also provide for feeding to a padded-down microphone input on our mixer. When needed, we can plug in a UREI limiter (such as when taping "uncontrollable" rock music groups) and a program-line equalizer for "sweetening." The painstaking effort and costly flexibility we built into our sound system has paid off time and time again in high directors' satisfaction (via time saved) and reduced technicians' frustration and tension.

### The Maintenance Area

Due to lack of space, the maintenance area ended up in the rear corner of the control room. This turned out rather well because Maintenance now has easy access to Video,

Station Sync and other pulses, besides waveform, monochrome and color-pix monitors, without having to run extra cables or purchase other equipment. It has the necessary test equipment including a unique, inexpensive Ramko in-circuit transistor checker, Hewlett Packard and ac and dc VTVMs, plus a Leader Instruments dual-trace 10 MHz oscilloscope which can check everything including the quadruplex VTR. One highly useful tool is a BNC-plug removal-insertion device made by Trompeter Electronics. In high density video patchbays, most of which use BNC plugs on the rear of the video jacks, and with other compact equipment such as distribution amplifiers stacked nearby, it is worth one's life to attempt to get a hand in there to remove or reconnect a cable. This inexpensive, simple tool does it quickly, surely...and effortlessly!

**Video Control**

Atop the three video racks, colored red, green, and blue respectively from left to right, representing the three primary TV colors, we have a large Admiral video monitor fed by a small Panasonic surveillance camera. This permits all control-room personnel to check placement of everything and everyone on stage and eliminates the need of a costly and wasteful control-room window. Next to it is a Standard Electric timer, more convenient to all concerned than a hand-held stopwatch. The control-room telephone is also there, plus a separate interfone linking Control Room with Office, Stage, Telecine/VTR, and Dressing Rooms. This independent interfone is far more useful, and less costly, than "telco" equipment, and was British-made by Modern Telephone Company.

Figure 8-3 details the placement of all video control and monitoring facilities. The circuit block-diagram and the positions of each piece of equipment in the racks were changed (on paper) about a dozen times before a satisfactory compromise was achieved. Since our studio must be able to quickly "go mobile," compactness, plus minimal interrack cable disconnect-reconnecting was mandatory. We selected three Stantron 52 in. racks on casters, after determining that not only would they be able to house everything but, more importantly, we should have all necessary equipment at a height convenient to all operating personnel. The racks are clamped together but are easily separated for moving.

We did something unorthodox that gave us both operating efficiency and physical compactness. We took turrets that normally are placed on top of desk-consoles and mounted them vertically on the center and righthand racks. While they protrude very little (crucial to our mobility) they provide the viewability and usability necessary to efficient operation. Already others have begun to copy this unique layout. I hope you will consider it.

Our setup, being fully professional, calls for a crew somewhat larger than some nonbroadcasters might have to "make do" with. The vision mixer (often mislabeled "technical director" or "T.D.") sits at the right-hand rack and operates the video switcher. The "shader" who "rides" camera gain and quality control throughout production, and who also operates patching and the lighting remote-control unit, sits at the left-hand rack. The show director, who may be on our staff or furnished by the client, sits between the shader and vision mixer. One audioman can normally handle all audio, including disc and tape, unless there are many tricky cues. Completing the crew are a telecine/VTR

Fig. 8-3. Meticulous attention to design permits placement of substantial amount of equipment in compact space. (Courtesy Telaudio Centre. Photo by Don Lauritzen.)

operator in the Telecine/VTR room; and of course, as many cameramen as are needed.

Depending on the production, we might have to bring in an electrician, a lighting director, grips, and set constructors. In any event, exclusive of the stage crew, a full complement of production personnel would number about eight. It is often suggested that we eliminate the shader and run the cameras on "automatic." Experience has shown that not only does this deliver pictures of far less than optimum quality, but also that the shader can be kept very busy and useful with tasks other than his duties of camera quality control. Incidentally, we use the fine "Porta-Pattern" camera-test charts, which we keep just "off-screen" but still under the illumination of the stage luminaires. Thus the shader can ask any cameraman during production to take a fast shot of the camera setup chart in the event that his camera is in need of minor adjustment during a show—which is often the case with even the most expensive cameras.

The shader's rack, going from bottom to top, is filled with equipment. Two color sync generators include color phaselock (genlock) inputs. A sync changeover permits instant switching from one sync generator to the other in case of failure. A luminance and chrominance control with either manual or automatic operation is included. On top of it is a black-burst-and-test patterns generator. All the foregoing equipment is made by Lenco. Above are two TeleMation test-signal generators, side-by-side, with space for one more. They are ten-step staircase and multiburst. These are followed by a row of 12 Dynair video and pulse distribution amplifiers with power supply. We have a spare VDA and a PDA in this array, plus a spare power supply on the shelf. Above the DAs is the electronics of the Dynair remote-controlled video switcher. Then come 52 Trompeter video jacks, an Ultra Audio chroma keyer and 52 more jacks. Sufficient patching is the secret of video versatility, and, as a consequence, production success.

Control units for the three Shibaden Plumbicon cameras are above the patchbays. And finally we have the remote-control units for the Zei-Mark telecine multiplexer. These too are operated by the shader. When these video racks are away on location, the telecine operates under "local" control, as will be discussed in the final chapter. The vision mixer, director, shader, telecineman, and cameraman all have Soundolier headsets, all of which are equipped with microphone on−off switches to eliminate unnecessary sound pickup, as usually only the director should be talking.

The director has, at his immediate command, monitors for the three live cameras and the Shibaden telecine vidicon camera, the latter's CCU being in Telecine and controlled by the Telecine/VTR operator. As will also be explained later, this CCU must be located with the telecine equipment, although it normally receives its drive pulses from the control room. Adjacent to each camera's video monitor is a waveform monitor, as we *never* rely on inaccurate meters for checking camera output. These waveform-pix combo monitors are standard Ultra Audio Products units and can easily be seen by both the shader and the vision-mixer, as well as by the director. Built-in tally lights on the UAP units permit everyone to see which camera is "up" (being "taken").

In the director's turret are two Panasonic 5 in. monochrome monitors, one of which is a spare for a sixth video source, if needed; the other is for Preview. The monitor contained in the third location was removed and the space was used to install a director's paging microphone—which is accessible to the vision-mixer as well. It contains a built-in on−off switch. Directly behind it is a Dynair "Mini-Fade." This device contains a fader that dissolves from one source to another. As you know, color television requires a source of pure black (black burst) to be fed to an input on the switcher in order to accomplish pure fades-to-black since you cannot split your faders and fade to "nothing" (except on a few switchers specifically designed to permit this). The trouble here is that you must sacrifice one of the few sorely-needed switcher inputs and relegate it to accept the black burst as its source. Not wanting to waste a precious and costly input in this fashion, we feed black burst to input-A and the video switcher output to input-B on the mini-fader. Our fades-to-black are then done on the mini-fader while we have up to six picture sources feeding the switcher. At any time we can patch black burst to the switcher, if desired.

Moving to the vision-mixer's rack, we encounter at the top a waveform-pix combo monitor for a monochrome titling camera that produces either black-on-white pix, or more importantly, reversed white-on-black video. This gives us titles that can be typed or lettered cheaply, then superimposed over other pictures. Below this display is a pair of Ultra Audio Products waveform monitors. The unit on the right is tied in with the World Video Inc. broadcast-grade color 12 in. monitor directly below it. It is equipped for individual H and V delay when switched-in by the user. This pair of monitors is not permanently connected anywhere, but may be patched anywhere—such as to any camera's output, switcher output, mini-fader output, procamp output, VTR output, etc. In this way we minimize our investment in costly color precision monitors.

The left-hand waveform monitor is our normal preview WFM, but connected to its input we've added a vertical 12-button push-switch, through which the vision mixer can make instant checks on the most important parts of the system. The inputs selectable are: CAMERA 1. CAM 2. CAM 3. TELECINE. TITLER. PATCHBAY JACK 1. JACK 2. STEP. PROCAMP. MULTIBURST. PROGRAM. PREVIEW. It is customarily left in PREVIEW position, and it is helpful to have a preview-line WFM to check output level on special effects being set up.

In the turret below the color monitor is the video-switcher panel controlling six synchronous (all switching is of composite video) sources and five nonsynchronous sources. Future equipment acquistions go in the blank spaces below the turrets.

All in all, the control room is fully equipped, but incredibly compact, yet there is room for expansion. We conclude in the subject next chapter with details of the Telecine/VTR room and its capabilities.

# Chapter 9

# An Economical Layout
# that Puts it All Together

In the previous chapters, we detailed the soundstage and the control room of a complete color teleproduction center built around so-called "bottom-of-the-line" broadcast-quality equipment. In this Chapter, we discuss the Telecine/VTR room. We house this equipment not only in its own room, but in one that is soundproof as well because of its nearness to the stage and control room. The bulky size of the several pieces of equipment makes a separate room an attractive choice; the disconcerting noise emanating from motors and moving mechanisms make the separate room a necessity. The soundproofing, incidentally, further serves to reduce the noise within the room itself. In short, it is a fairly "dead" room, which minimizes operator distraction and fatigue.

The studio floor plan shows that the room is small—6½ ft × 10½ ft. Most of the equipment in it can be seen in Fig. 9-1. At the right is the RCA quadruplex video tape recorder. This is a colorized low-band machine combining one remarkable feature normally not available to helical-scan VTR users. It includes "pix-lock," which means that this VTR's playback can be locked to "station sync" (master sync from the control room). Because of this, we do not have to "genlock" our station sync to the VTR's playback. Instead, the VTR's playback "genlocks" to station sync—just as the studio cameras do.

Consequently, the videotape being played can be handled as though it were another camera. And, since we switch composite video, as all broadcasters now do (contrasted to synchronous but noncomposite camera control in most industrial-grade installations), we treat

Fig. 9-1. Noisy equipment is located in soundproofed Telecine/VTR room to cut down on distractions. (Courtesy Telaudio Centre. Photo by Don Lauritzen.)

videotape playback as just another synchronous source. This makes it possible to achieve all sorts of flexibility (such as fades and special effects) when integrating a prerecorded tape into a new program. You might thus consider the playback tape as being much like cine film. Of course, we could genlock the VTR, which is great with quadruplex but not very satisfactory with helical-scan sources because of their very unstable sync.

Regrettably, you pay a high price for this capability for not only is a quadruplex VTR a costly purchase, but upkeep and operating expenses are high. The quadruplex operator must be experienced and the quadruplex maintenance technician highly skilled. Without this, you may get mediocre recordings and abominable playback of good recordings. But quadruplex is capable of producing videotapes noticeably superior to anything except for those few tapes made on the most expensive helicals which are time-base corrected and literally "babied" by outstanding, conscientious, dedicated technicians.

Quadruplex VTRs require both air-pressure and vacuum systems. Vacuum systems configure the tape properly as it passes the video head(s), and are usually located within the machine. An external air-pressure system is used to turn the air-bearing quadruplex heads. These compressors vibrate a great deal and are very noisy, so they are placed away from the machine, interconnecting them with a long hose. The quadruplex was raised onto giant casters to make it easily movable into a van. There is one more crucial requirement of quadruplex VTRs: they like to operate in rooms of about 70° F temperature and 45% relative humidity. Failing this, head life deteriorates rapidly . . . and it costs at least $1000 for head refurbishing, to say nothing of the downtime. Also, 20A of power should be availabe to the VTR.

Returning to Fig. 9-1, we see a Zei-Mark optical multiplexer sporting an Eastman 16mm projector on the left input and a 2 × 2 slide projector at center. We have no source on the right-hand input at present; perhaps ultimately we will use Super-8. Obscured by the VTR is the Shibaden vidicon Telecine camera, in front of which is a Shibaden neutral-density filter wheel which quickly and automatically adjusts to compensate for variations in the density of different cine films and especially 35mm slides. The projectors and the optical changeovers are controlled both at the multiplexer and in the control room. We've also installed a Zei-Mark "tel-op" assembly in front of the 16mm projector on the multiplexer. This unique device permits the Telecine to display an illuminated title card, or other graphics, when properly placed in line with the tel-op lens. Thus, a costly studio camera is not needed for such assignments. Hanging from the mirror assembly is a Soundolier headset which can be plugged into the camera or its CCU, whichever is most convenient at the time.

Although the quadruplex video recorder includes its own waveform and pulse cross monitors (and, as I've said before, if quadruplex machines see fit to include pulse cross monitoring of tape playback, helical-scan machines need monitoring of it even more so), we have two Ultra Audio Products PCMs, are two RCA waveform monitors bought surplus as discontinued items, formerly used by

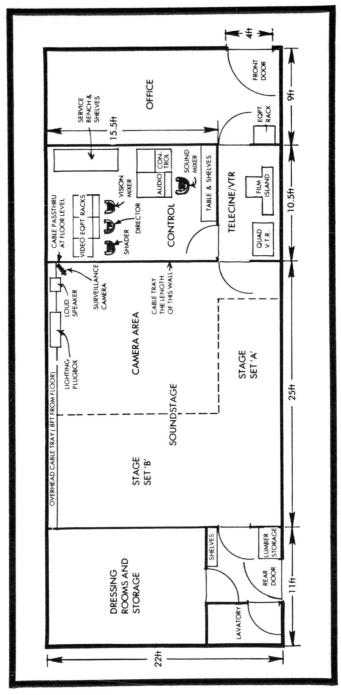

Fig. 9-2. Floor plan of studio.

NBC. Although they are patchable to any portion of the circuit, one waveform and pulse cross monitor pair normally checks VTR output, especially inasmuch as the VTR's WFM is usually switched to monitor other portions of the VTR's circuitry, while the other monitor Telecine exhibitions. The rack also houses the camera's CCU, which gets it drive pulses from the control room. When the control room is away "on location," a Lenco changeover unit switches to another sync generator located in an inexpensive California Chassis Co. telecine rack. This permits it to function independently of the main control room whenever desired.

We have a fine Cohu monochrome sync generator that nearly became "obsolete" with the advent of color. Not wanting to lose our investment in this costly device, we obtained a "colorizer" from Modern Video Engineering Co., which turns any properly equipped monochrome unit into a top-flight full-color device. It adds the required black burst and color subcarrier outputs. In an inexpensive Switchcraft jackpanel, we have installed the needed complement of audio jacks, plus the necessary Trompeter video jacks. While there is much to be said for so-called routing switchers, jackbays are more versatile, more compact, and less costly. A well-designed patchbay is a *must* for flexible and efficient studio operations, and is well worth the sometimes *frightening* investment, Still, our video bays account for about 1% of the total studio cash outlay.

Connected to the patchbay are the inputs and outputs of three distribution amplifiers in the handy and economical Dynair "mini" series—video, pulse, and audio. This permits us to transfer film, videotape (and live material too) to up to four other recorders, usually JVC ¾ in. cassette or ½ in. reel-to-reel. When we get requests to dub film to videocassette or other helical formats, we dub film to quadruplex and then quadruplex to helical. The DAs facilitate this. We also have a Dynair 12-input composite video switcher-fader for use, as needed, in Telecine/VTR operation. This unit serves as a spare in case of failure of our control-room production switcher. While it does not offer the flexibility of the production switcher, substituting it in an emergency would save the show, even though it would take a half-hour's time to do so. When you offer facilities for hire, you must have available considerable protection against equipment failure—via patching and spares.

We also have a Conrac demodulator (TV tuner) in the rack for receiving off-the-air programs for clients desiring "air-checks," such as advertising agencies, actors, sponsors, and talent agencies. Finally, we have a World Video portable receiver-monitor for use in Telecine/VTR or elsewhere. Audio is monitored via Acoustic Research amplifier and speaker.

**In Summary**

We feel the studio complex we have described not only represents the ultimate in budget-conscious teleproduction facilities, but it truly reflects all of the "rules" of design that we have espoused so often. It's an example of "making do" with limited funds.

# Chapter 10

## Audio For Video

It is nothing short of *criminal* the way so many CATV and CCTV studios neglect their audio. Audio is treated virtually as an "also ran" or even a "necessary evil" to be paid for out of whatever funds are left in the budget after video facilities are completed. Upon seeing this happen time and time again, one begins to understand why.

First, there is the possibility of oversight—after all, the glamour is in video and the cost of audio is minimal in comparison with video. Secondly, there is a positive lack of understanding of how complex quality, flexible audio systems might become. It should not be assumed that audio is simple just because most video products contain more circuitry than do audio amplifiers. Finally, there appears to be a complete underestimation of the customizing required for comprehensive audio. This is due possibly to the fact that an entire video system can be assembled from "off-the-shelf" products, whereas such flexibility in prefabricated audio products is nonexistent.

### No Cost Ground Rules

There are no rules governing the cost ratio of audio to total studio equipment outlay. A $200,000 complete color production facility should probably include $5000 worth of audio. But a studio costing half as much may still require a $5000 audio investment. While it might seem far-fetched at the moment, *stereo* audio facilities may soon be required. Already videocassettes contain two audio tracks; in the near future broadcast television VTRs may be equipped with two top-grade audio channels for stereo multiplexing (aural FM transmitters are capable of accepting such feeds).

Most commonly overlooked, or at least underestimated, is the need for audition, cueing, and playback capabilities. In order to achieve full audio flexibility and versatility it is necessary that audition, playback, and cueing circuitry bypass the basic system used for the recording process. For example, VTR (audio portion) playback need not—and should not—be fed through an input on the mixing console (except perhaps, but not always, in the case of dubbing). Instead it should go directly to the monitor amplifier. Disc turntable cueing, as well as prerecorded audio tapes auditioning (when such tapes are to be integrated into a videotape production) must bypass the mixing console. Why? Well, for one thing, the audioman must be able to audition anything he wants while a show is in progress (the director may wish to also). Secondly, why tie up one of the mixer's inputs for, say, playback of the tape being produced, when that input is needed for use with some other source? Finally, you must be able to have instant audio playback at the push of a button, and avoid having to make repeated reconnections whenever the director wants to screen material previously produced.

**List the Sources**

To create a flexible audio system it is necessary to list the *sources of sound*, then list those who must hear them and under what conditions. While few industrial-grade studios would require every capability, here is a list of most of the sources that you would have to contend with: microphones, one or more disc turntables, cartridge tape players, reel-to-reel audio tape players, VTR audio (from the VTR used in recording the current production and perhaps from another machine containing a previously recorded videotape), Telecine (motion picture film audio—usually single-system but possibly interlocked double-system in a pretentious studio), "off-the-air" TV audio from a demodulator, remote "telco" lines, and lines from your other studios in the building.

Now consider what is to be done with these sources. First, they must be connectable to the master audio mixing "console." Secondly, they must be capable of being auditioned in the control room. Thirdly, one or more of them must be playable in the control room (while some other things are being simultaneously auditioned); and finally, one or more must be playable to the performers on the soundstage. (You don't want actors to have to leave the stage and enter the control room area to hear and see program playback.) Furthermore, you may have to feed "cue" or instructions to one or more actors, via headphones, during a production. Such apparent redundance of communications circuits allows for correction of unforeseen circumstances which often occur during a performance.

In an eariler chapter of this book, we described a sophisticated color teleproduction plant at Telaudio Centre, Burbank, where it was shown that the audio was given as much thought as the video. Let us consider that audio system in detail and see how it encompasses all of the "rules" set forth. Figure 10-1 is a block diagram of this system. Carefully note that in contradistinction to video, audio equipment offers various levels and impedances. No attempt has been made to indicate these specifically here, because it depends upon the specific brands of equipment chosen. It will be necessary for you to match impedances and levels via appropriate transformers and amplifiers, after studying the manufacturers' specifications.

A word of caution. Unless you are on a very slim budget, try to use all *professional* audio equipment instead of consumer-grade products, because the latter just won't be reliable for long. Besides, consumer products usually do not offer "studio" impedances and levels, and it will cost you time and money to adapt them. Further, although patchbays are tedious to wire, *plan on them* because they are a "lifesaver" in time, money, space, and flexibility. It also goes without saying that, whenever possible, audio equipment should be housed separately and away from the video. It should be operated by an audio specialist.

## Consider A Peak-Limiter And Program-Equalizer

Two pieces of equipment, not normally considered in nonbroadcast television studios, are very worthy of

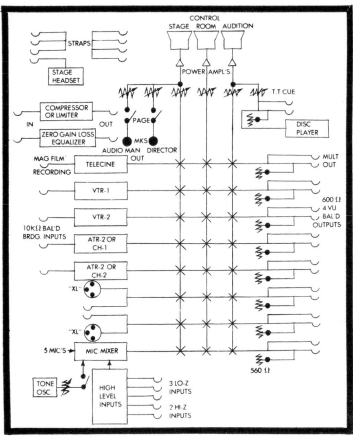

Fig. 10-1. Well planned audio system with pushbutton monitor setup and patching permits speedy, efficient operation. Has capability of doing many things simultaneously, without interfering with each other.

mention. The first is a peak-limiter. Inexperienced audiomen often find it impossible to manually exercise adequate control over sound levels. The performer is either speaking too softly or too loudly. The busy audioman may be unable to effectively "ride gain" on this. The limiter will do it automatically, and is especially useful when recording musical groups. You can arrange to patch-in the limiter as needed, or you can keep it permanently connected to the mixer's output. The second "lifesaver" is a program-equalizer. It is very handy for cutting out unexpected hum, for minimizing sibilance and also record scratch, and for boosting certain frequencies such as a voice or musical instrument that sounds thin. By having your equalizer patchable, you attain the added versatility of connecting it as desired to, say, the film's audio only, or the audio tape recorder's output only, or the disc playback only, while *not* affecting the frequency response of the entire composite program audio coming out of the mixer and feeding the VTR. Of course, you can always patch it to the mixer's (master program line) output. To achieve maximum flexibility, all circuits into which an equalizer might be inserted must be of the same impedance and level!

In Fig. 10-2 we see the primary portion of the audio-control assembly. In this particular instance, the audioman was given remote control of the telecine by placing this equipment in the desk arm of the console. Patching is at the top so that the cords may be pushed up and out of the way. Most convenient to the audioman is the 5-input (plus master gain control) microphone mixer including VU meter. Note the designation-strip for penciling-in what each mix position is controlling. Above this are program and preview monochrome monitors so the audioman can clearly see what's going on and what's coming next. Last but definitely not least is the Setup

Fig. 10-2. Elaborate audio facilitates may be placed in a small area but separate from the video. Give the audioman his own control room if you have the space and the budget.

panel—the heart of the system and the portion that makes audio flexibility a reality—even more so than the patchbay.

Figure 10-3 details the Setup panel, which was designed (with painstaking care) after all the criteria mentioned earlier were evaluated. It is truly an audioman's (and director's) "dream." The audio is now *more* versatile than the video and can be changed and adapted infinitely more rapidly, to accommodate any requirement and any piece of temporary or supplementary equipment. Let's see how.

There are three power amplifiers housed in the base of the audio console. One feeds the control-room monitor loudspeaker, the second feeds the sound-stage speaker and the third drives the control-room audition speaker. Each of the three monitor systems is fed by a row of eight pushbutton switches with the button being illuminated only when depressed. "Lockout" prevents more than one button in any row from being depressed at a time. Each set of buttons can select anything while the other two systems are simultaneously selecting the same source or, obviously, *any* (other) sources. Everything feeding these switchbanks is high level ($-20$ to $+8$dB), $600\Omega$ balanced. To the left of each switchbank is the volume control for its power amplifier/loudspeaker.

Because disc-record playback is not something normally fed to all monitors, its auditioning (cue) is connected via a gain control to only the control room's audition amplifier and not to the three rows of pushbuttons. This control is labeled TT-Q. Below it is a PAGE gain control and the paging microphone's on—off lever key. This is to permit the audioman to page the soundstage via the stage monitor amplifier. The director, who sits at the video racks with the Vision Mixer, also has a paging microphone. Note that the audioman's microphone is inset on the Setup panel.

There are five high-level mix position's—three low impedance and two hi-Z. None of the high-level sources going to the pushbuttons are connected to the mixer's inputs. Instead, all sources terminate at the patchbay. The audioman then patches any sources he's going to use and *only* those sources) to any of the three lo-Z or two hi-Z mix positions. These five high-level inputs are more than enough for whatever sources will be needed for any particular show. Independent of what's patched in, any one of the three monitor systems then selects what it wants to hear—FILM. VTR-1. VTR-2. ATR-1. ATR-2. AUX-1. AUX-2. or the output of the MIXER. By referring to Fig. 10-1 and Fig. 10-3, the infinite flexibility achieved becomes clear.

Lastly, note the white knob-and-twist key to its left. The key turns on a 1 kHz oscillator within the mixer, and the knob controls the oscillator's output level. By setting this to zero on the VU meter's scale, all audio equipment (VTRs, ATRs, telephone lines) being fed by the console may have their levels set in synchronization with that of the mixer. It was mentioned earlier that an actor may have to receive cue information from an audio source during production. In this instance he would wear headphones wired to a jack on the patchbay. A patchcord would then connect whatever source is to be fed to the actor.

Throughout the show the audioman may be required to make various changes, occasionally via the patchbay and frequently through use of the pushbuttons, not only for himself but also for the needs of the director and the performers. To give an example, the show may require four microphones, audio-tape play, disc play, and 16mm film integration. The microphones are plugged into the mixer's first four MIC inputs. Phono is patched to high-level INPUT. 1. Film is patched in input CONTROL. 2. ATR (audio tape recorder playback) would be patched to INPUT. 3. Perhaps the narrator will be required to begin talking immediately after the audio-tape playback segment ceases, so his headphones are patched so that he can hear the ATR's

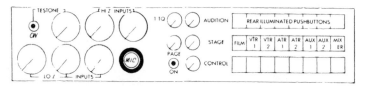

Fig. 10-3. Detail of setup panel which, when coupled with patchbay, makes any setup for recording, playback or both, convenient and in-stantaneous.

output—*not* the mixer's output because the mixer's output contains (distracting) background music and other actor's voices.

During the show the director may wish to quickly audition the film's audio, or the film's video or the audioman may wish to audition film to confirm that the projector is properly cued (and threaded). The audioman will also have to cue his disc record to the proper groove. After completion of videotaping the actors and control-room personnel may have to be fed videotape playback (sound and pix) in order to review their performance. This would then be "punched up" on the Stage's monitor speaker. Perhaps during playback the audioman will have to audition (in the control room only) a disc, audio tape or motion picture film that is to be used in taping the next show or segment. He can, and *must* be able to do so simultaneously without interfering with the aforementioned playback. This system makes all this possible—and with ease.

Hopefully it can be seen that by making the audio facilities sufficiently "complex," the net effect will be smoother, quicker, easier, broader, better, and more effective audio for video.

# Chapter 11

## Audio-Video Interlock and TV Tape Editing

In the early days of "talkies," motion picture synchronous sound was not only recorded on a separate medium (disc) from the visuals, but was played separately in the theatres. That is, the disc was played on a turntable which was synchronized to the projection of the images. In fact, the now-standard 33⅓ rpm speed was created because a 16-in. diameter disc played at this speed could record a long enough period to match the length of a reel of 35mm movie film. Later technology made it possible to combine sound and image recording on one piece of film. Magnetic-videotape recording permitted both aural and video signals to be captured simultaneously.

It is now possible to interlock two (or more) video tape recorders, or video and audio tape recorders, by "slaving" one or more machines to the master recorder. There are two ways to achieve synchronization, which one might call *simple interlock* and *complex interlock*.

### Control Tone For Simple Interlock

In simple interlock we encounter two conditions, which we might refer to as *synchronous recording* or *recording add-on*. In the former situation, audio is recorded separately but simultaneously with video. A case in point would be the recording of a rock concert on a 16- or 24-track audio machine while simultaneously videotaping the affair. The audio can be subsequently mixed down to one, two, or four channels. Later, such a program could be aired with stereo sound by simulcasting in conjunction with an FM station. Interestingly, this technique raises a legal question which as of this moment has not been tested: If a TV program's audio is carried in stereo with one audio channel being the telecaster's aural frequency, while the other audio channel is carried on an FM station, then obviously both the telecaster and the FMer are guilty of carrying degraded audio because each is carrying only a portion of the total audio available. In order to overcome the legal ramifications of this, the telecaster should carry both stereo audio channels combined on his aural transmitter; while the FMer should be broadcasting *both* stereo channels (in stereo, of course) instead of just one. Then the radio listener could hear all the audio without any television, while the televiewer could turn off his TV's audio and listen to FM radio—stereo or mono—for all the sound of the show; or he could hear all the audio via his TV set, whichever he prefers.

In such synchronous and simultaneous recording, a tone is "laid down" on both the VTRs audio channel and on one track of the multitrack audio tape recorder (ATR). There should also be start marks (a flash of light picked up by a camera and videotaped simultaneously with a "beep" on the audio). Then, when the machines are up to speed, another "bloop" and "beep" could be recorded. When the playback operator has started the machines at the sync marks, yet sees that the "bloop" and "beep" at the full-speed points are not quite together, he speeds up the ATR, or slows it down, via variable speed control on this machine, until synchronization is achieved. An ingenious audio recorder has recently been introduced which makes synchronization "child's play," Fig. 11-1. This multitrack audio recorder, now available in 16-, 24- and even 40-channel versions, will remain synchronized to virtually any other stable video or audio recorder. It does so by constantly comparing the frequency of the control tone on the master recorder, usually the VTR, to the frequency of the control-tone recorded on one of its many audio tracks. Variation in speed of either machine causes a frequency difference which actuates the speed change servomechanism in this ATR. The result is instantaneous continuing speed correction to maintain synchronization.

The recorder just described has a far easier job in speed control and interlock than conventional machines

Fig. 11-1. 16-track capstanless-drive studio audio recorder provides easy video intersync. (Courtesy Stephens Electronics.)

having an intersync feature because this recorder has no drive-capstan system. That's right, the tape is pulled through by the takeup motor, a device originally developed for aerospace use which operates on less than 5V and requires a tiny amount of current. In fact, an entire 24-track recorder, including transport and amplifiers, can be carried like a suitcase by one man. In nonvideo applications, such as in recording studios, this machine can seek out and locate any point in the recording desired by the operator. Furthermore, contrary to conventional ATRs, there is no "overshoot" during *search*; that is, the machine knows when it is approaching the desired spot and slows down in advance—just as you do when you drive your car up to a stop sign.

*Add-on* recording in which audio and video are synchronized is easy with this device. Suppose, for example, a vocalist is to be videotaped lip-syncing to his previously recorded music and voice—but the audio tape has no sync tone on it because it was previously recorded elsewhere for, say, disc record release. No matter, because this recorder's drive system permits it to synchronize to a 60 Hz control track tone recorded on the VTR. This becomes the *reference* for the ATR whose speed is controlled by a 60 Hz frequency injected into its logic system.

### Time Code Reference For Complex Interlock

The same system that makes *search* possible also makes possible interlock of this sound recorder with a video tape recorder, regardless of their respective starting points. In fact, the ATR we've described will find correct synchronization regardless of where it or the VTR began—provided both machines have had recorded on their tapes what is known as the SMPTE (Society of Motion Picture & TV Engineers) edit code. This all-encompassing system provides for the laying down of 80 binary bits per TV frame (2400/second) to identifying every frame by hour, minute, second, and frame count. Furthermore, it makes no difference whether the time recorded is elapsed time (beginning with zero at the start of the tape) or time of day.

Fig. 11-2. Compact edit code generator & reader make possible tape search, interlock of machines and videotape electronic editing. (Courtesy Stephens Electronics.)

The only thing that matters is that the code is recorded, as generated by a device such as shown in Fig. 11-2.

The system accommodates the full 24-hour day on its clock and logic system. The heart of the system is the code reader (receiving its "feed" from the VTR) and the difference converter (actuating an *enabler* that varies the speed of the slave machine—the ATR, for example—until the time codes of each machine are identical). It continues to maintain this synchronization until stopped or until one tape runs out. Figure 11-3 shows a building block array of edit-code readers and programmers, a well thought-out system allowing the smallest possible initial investment, if desired, yet one which can grow (to many tens of thousands of dollars) to create a sophisticated multimachine editing and synchronizing system.

Fig. 11-3. EECO building-block system of editors and synchronizers allows user to begin with small and expand to sophisticated multi-machine control. (Courtesy Electronic Engineering Co. of Calif.)

Fig. 11-4. Vidicue editor features avoidance of precoding entire videotape length. (Courtesy Datatron.)

### Time Code Makes Electronic Video Editing Practical

If you've ever encountered the frustrations in trying to "punch" in and out of a scene for videotape *insert editing*, or if you've ever had to *assemble* a production *electronically*, you know you're ready for a machine to do the timing for you. In Fig. 11-4 we see another such device, this one offering an outstanding feature, called "Jam-Sync" by the manufacturer. Jam-Sync precludes the need to lay down the edit code on the entire length of the fresh tape being used for assembling a show from other master tapes. (This also saves headwear and tapewear because it is now necessary only to record about three minutes of edit code on the raw stock.) Jam-Sync also picks up where you left off on stop-and-go live productions that do not run continuously.

The cost-conscious production house that must use helical-scan VTRs due to budget limitations, may not be excited at the thought of having to spend $5000 to $15,000 for an electronic editor/synchronizer. But, sad to say, it is the user of helical machines that needs electronic editing most of all—for cutting and splicing physically is virtually out of the question. Electronic editors also allow you to preview your planned edits, make sure they're the way you want them, then order your machines to go ahead and make the "cut." Naturally, your VTRs must be capable of remote control and must incorporate capstan-servo editing capability so as to actuate on the vertical interval. They must have all this is in addition to an audio or cue channel to accept the SMPTE edit code information.

# Chapter 12

## Mobile Madness

It seems as though it's the dream of every cableman, ETV–ITV operator, and industrial studio producer to have at his disposal a beautifully equipped video van for those exciting "location" teleproductions. Well, before you invest in such a unit, you'd better consider what's in store for you should you rush into an area "where angels fear to tread." There are so many unforeseen ramifications and drawbacks to a permanent mobile unit that unless you have very frequent use for one you'd be best to consider the alternatives—again and again.

The van, itself, poses a myriad of problems. If you go for compactness in order to save money, you end up with a Volkswagen-style truck. You discover that you can't stand up in it; it won't support the weight of very much color video equipment; there's little room for an ac generator, and perhaps not for air conditioning either (which you and your equipment will be desperate for in the summer); your delicate and costly equipment will have to be pushed up against a wall and thus will be severely damaged in the event of an accident; and, with the equipment so placed, maintenance and connecting to it become a nightmare.

Still not dissuaded? Well, wait till you have to take the van—any van—in for servicing. You suddenly find that you've lost the use of the equipment, too, during this period. You also find that there's a strong chance your equipment will be stolen or damaged while the vehicle is being serviced. Have you been reading the increasing number of reports of stolen video equipment, particularly equipment locked in a truck?

Any designer or user of TV network mobile units will tell you that even the largest of the giant buses or semis is never found to be large enough in actual use. So, armed with this fact, you consider investing in a "bread truck" type vehicle, such as a "Vanette," "Metro," or "Step-Van." At least you can stand up (if you're under six feet tall) in one of these, provided it doesn't rock too much as you move about. But watch out for how these vehicles sway on the road and the fact that they get terribly top-heavy. Hopefully, too, you have enough money to pay for one of these, and for all the optional accessories that you'll definitely need. Watch out also for equipment you'll need to meet OSHA requirements.

Had any experience with generators for use in powering your equipment out in the field? Not only will you need one rated at least 50% higher than the amount of current your equipment draws, but wait until you encounter the grounding problems—hum and inexplicable electric shocks. By the way, these conditions will exist in *any* vehicle, even if you're connected to nearby permanent house current instead of mobile generators. Be prepared for substantial generator noise and vibration. And don't forget that in addition to power for your video equipment you'll need much more for air conditioning and the portable lights—which will no doubt have to be located as far away from the van as the cameras will be—maybe much farther.

What's the answer, then? My principal answer is: If you don't have need for mobility on at least two occasions a week, don't buy a truck—pick up a phone and explain your requirements to a truck rental agency. That's right; why tie up "big bucks" in your own van when you can rent a truck with electric tailgate for relatively nominal sums? Furthermore, don't plan to use the truck as a control room unless you have no choice. Instead, use it for transportation only and use available space at the remote location to serve as a control room. Not only will this solve many of the aforementioned problems, it will almost always require shorter lengths of expensive microphone, monitor, and *very* expensive camera cables. Finally, this same equipment serves as your studio at home base, as well (assuming, of course, you are not so active as to require two complete video outfits).

If you're still "agin me" and you *must* buy a van, and operate from inside one, consider making it your *permanent* control room at your *home*, fixed studio. This may be more practical than buying two separate video systems, one fixed and one mobile. Whether or not you plan it this way, Fig. 12-1 shows a layout for a functional mobile video array. Note that it's built into one of the more rugged, more powerful, and more stable vans with separated cab that will comfortably seat three persons. This is preferable to the prettier walk-in United Parcel-type delivery trucks described earlier. These trucks will survive an accident better than the UPS type, too, besides being more suited to long distance and higher speed hauls. The absence of wheel-wells in this style of truck is also conducive to unimpaired equipment location at the most appropriate points in the load area.

Of primary importance is shock-mounting the cameras, for they do not travel well. We find that setting them on 8 in. thick foam rubber with 4 in. walls is effective, (Fig. 12-2). One of the TV networks that uses rather heavy cameras affixed a padded camera case to a hand-truck, one for each camera, which is a very effective method of storing the cameras and transporting them from the van to the point of use. Whereas rack equipment requires little vibration protection, you may wish to consider fastening the racks to the truck bed via shockmounts, which should be adequate protection for the waveform and video monitors therein. Portable VTRs are generally rugged enough to require scant protection, but you may wish to set them on shock-mounted flatbeds."

If you decide to "go first class" you're in for many hundreds, even thousands, of dollars in panelwork on the body, which should be of aluminum, rather than steel, for easier reworking and reduced weight, the latter essential for increasing the equipment payload capability by as much as 700 lbs. The inclusion of outside-access compartments, which must be securely locked, makes for the most convenient access to cameras, tripods, dollies, lights, microphones, stands, headsets, and monitors—that is, all

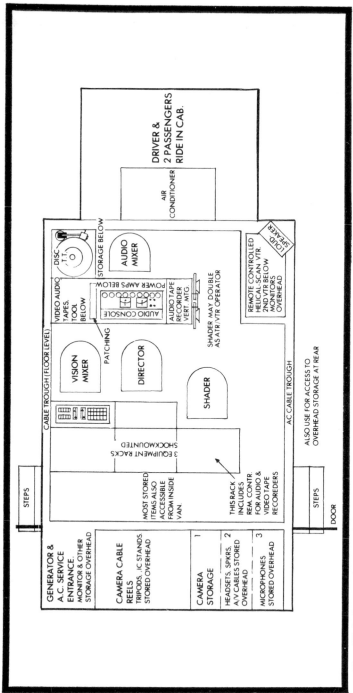

Fig. 12-1. Layout for a mobile van. Careful placement of generator and ac service entrance keeps noise down and power wiring away from A/V cables. For collision protection no equipment can be carried in rear walkway.

the equipment that must be used away from the van once it has arrived at the site. One costly consideration is the camera-cables that run from the control units (CCUs) to the plug on one end (for the CCU) and a panel-mounting receptacle on the other, permitting the cameras to be connected from the outside. The cost of this is substantial, considering the modest benefit in convenience it affords; thus you may prefer to have a trap door (cable port) through which to pass the camera cables for connection directly to their respective camera control units. You may wish to apply this same theory to *all* audio and video lines.

Choose a vehicle with four rear wheels for greater payload and stability. Furthermore, should one tire experience a blowout, the other three will provide considerable temporary protection. You are now in position to place your equipment to suit your taste, bearing in mind the load limits for each axle and the rule of thumb that the

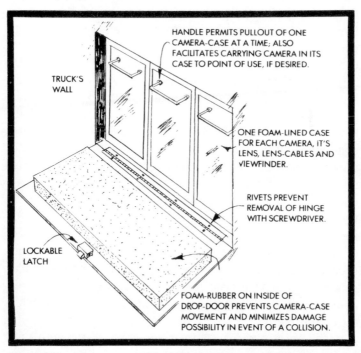

Fig. 12-2. Method of storing delicate camera in mobile van, with access from outside.

load on any axle should, during driving at least, be such that no more than 55% of the axle's load shall be on any side of center line of the van. This will improve cornering, for one thing. Be sure your vehicle, when completed, will pass governmental highway inspection requirements. Don't mount heavy objects more than halfway up the side of a wall, or your van may sway and lose some controllability. Purchase all heavy-duty accessories available. You may also wish to include automatic transmission, power steering and brakes. Consult the truck-chassis dealer to determine who makes a body for it that is most appropriate to your needs. Perhaps you can select not only a body having features you deem appropriate but also a bodymaker who will custom-build the compartments you want.

Ground your equipment racks to the frame of the van and make provision for grounding the van to either earth, via a ground rod, or a cold-water pipe at the remote site. Carry two flashlights, preferably the heavy-duty kind using lantern batteries; plenty of flares; road cones to keep people away from the van and the delicate, expensive cables; plastic camera covers; umbrellas on stands to shield cameras from sun and rain; tools; voltohmmeter; tape and the many other knicknacks your experience has proven necessary. Be sure to carry spare cables of all kinds, as a crucial one is bound to fail. Keep delicate equipment away from the truck's rear and side walls, to minimize chance of damage in the event of an accident. Rig the interior of the load area with battery (the van's) operated worklights and ac-powered lighting. If you plan to use a generator to power your equipment, provision for shock mounting, cooling, noise reduction, and changeover to external house current should be discussed and coordinated with the generator supplier. Rather than a single, very high-powered generator, two smaller units may be more practical. Install a second battery in parallel with the engine battery.

Make provision for 230V service entry to the van; and for an air conditioner capable of cooling the interior to 40 degrees below that of the exterior—with the equipment *on.*

If you plan on having personnel occupy the interior during drive time, you'll need air conditioning powered by the vehicle itself. Mount a platform on the roof (the roof alone is probably not suitable for supporting a camera, tripod, perhaps lights, and one or two people) and you'll often have an excellent vantage point for teleproduction. Use a removable ladder to prevent unauthorized persons from gaining access to the roof. If you plan on having access to the heavy removable equipment from the outside, carry a ramp (known in the moving trades as a walk board) for those occasions when you have to bring heavy equipment in or out of the van. Otherwise you may be able to get along with a set or two of sturdy steps. If you don't have outside access to the removable equipment, then instead of a walk board, I'd use an electric tailgate and I'd also use a body equipped with full-width rear doors plus at least one side door. Windows are costly and unnecessary.

A five-gallon can of extra gasoline is a good investment; and look into liquefied propane gas as a form of fuel. Have a sign painter make you a couple of self-supporting sandwich boards, or similar weatherproof signs, announcing, "Caution—Delicate TV Cables—Keep Clear."

Finally, it is frequently more convenient to operate the audio equipment away from the van, just as the cameras are. This is often the case when doing productions in theatres and arenas, and in the case of sports events. Because of this you should make your low-level (microphones) mixer truly portable and even carry a portable loudspeaker and amplifier to substitute for headphones. The audioman may also need a video program monitor and an interfone headset for inter communication. You may wish to mount a paging loudspeaker on the roof of the van—very handy for giving instructions during (nearby) setup, production, and striking. It could also serve to carry program audio to interested persons, not only in production but also for the sound track in videotape playback.

# Chapter 13
## Practical Set-Lighting

First, let's define a few things: A lighting fixture is correctly called a *luminaire*. The word derives from the name of the Frenchman, Lumière, from whom we also get the terms *lumen* and even *illuminate*. Because the word luminaire is somewhat archaic, we'll usually refer to our lighting fixtures as *lights*. But the light source is not a bulb, but a *lamp*. A "klieglight" is a fixture made only by the Kliegl Brothers, and could apply to anything they make.

"Showbiz-oriented" columnists use the word indistriminately, just as many people call all brands of refrigerators Frigidaires, and all makes of record players Victrolas. Not to be outdone, Century Lighting Co. has trade-named their ellipsoidal lamp housings "Lekolite." Consequentially, innumerable users call all brands of ellipsoidals by that name—probably much to the chagrin of Century-Strand. Finally, the Fresnel light is anybody's fixture that incorporates a lens design created by still another Frenchman.

Britain's great physicist, Lord Kelvin, is immortalized via the use of his name in designating the color temperature of a lamp. Roughly speaking, the higher the color temperature rating of the lamp, the more efficient it is; i.e., the more output it delivers for a given amount of current drain. But one reason for not rushing out to buy these "wonder lamps" is that they often not only cost more than lesser-rated lamps, but also offer a much shorter life. For example, the series BTM 3200° K lamp rated at 100 hours of life costs the same as the BTL 3050° K lamp which lasts a whopping 500 hours. Considering the time wasted in purchasing and relamping, you're paying a pretty penny for the 3200° K efficiency. Later we shall attempt a compromise between the three critical considerations—economy, efficiency, and versatility.

While on the subject of color temperature, keep these facts in mind. Whereas artificial lighting is in the 3000° range, daylight is in the 5000° area and *increases* to possibly 8000° Kelvin under cloudy conditions. In this latter instance, although the color temperature is high, the intensity of the light will most likely be down, requiring "more iris" (larger lens openings—lower f-stops). Finally, the internationally proposed color temperature for color video is much "cooler" (bluer) on the monitor than it is in the studio where it is invariably redder in content.

Shortly we will explore, and perhaps "explode" what I call "the 3200° K myth." Meanwhile, let's look at Fig. 13-1 which offers some startling and revealing comparisons. The base row depicts the characteristics when operating any lamp at its specified rating. But, as shown in comparison A, if we were to take, say, a 3200° lamp and drop it to 3000° by dropping the voltage from 120 to 100, it would last 11 times as long and pull 25% less current. However, our enthusiasm is curbed when we observe that light output drops 45%. But suppose we used that 3150° lamp mentioned earlier and dimmed it down to 3000°? Via comparison B we see that we then get nearly double the life while losing only some 13° effective output. Consequently, by positioning the light properly we will p.obably avoid the need for another fixture (which would have been demanded had we dimmed a 3200° lamp); we avoid the additional air conditioning needed for large arrays of fixtures, and we avoid the extra wiring and plugging requirements for more luminaires. Finally, if we choose to, we can run the 3050°

| | General Electric Company Approximate Ratings | | | | |
| COMPAR-ISON | 1<br>°K CHANGE IN<br>COLOR TEMP. | 2<br>% LIGHT<br>OUTPUT | 3<br>% WATTS<br>DRAIN | 4<br>% RATED<br>LIFE | 5<br>SOCKET<br>VOLTAGE |
|---|---|---|---|---|---|
| BASE | 0 | 100 | 100 | 100 | 120 |
| A | −200 | 55 | 75 | 1100 | 100 |
| B | −50 | 87 | 94 | 190 | 115 |

Fig. 13-1. Lamp characteristic comparisons when under dimmer control.

Fig. 13-2. Remote-controlled 12-circuit dimmer with two-scene preset. (Courtesy Century-Strand.)

lamp at full voltage, giving us full light output while being so close to 3000° K as to make the difference unnoticeable.

But, you say, in all of the cases above we are not even running at 3200° K! Well, who says you have to? Not the camera makers! Most professional color television cameras are designed to accept 3000° (or higher) light. One of the reasons for this is to permit operation of lamps that have been *dimmed*, the dimming being for the purpose of achieving dramatic lighting effects—to say nothing of increasing lamp life and reducing power consumption. Now we see why the requirement of 3200° K is not really mandatory at all. So, if you cannot afford the luxury of a dimmer, why not at least use long-life 3050° lamps and set your camera's color-temperature control to 3000° K?

However, before you decide to discard the idea of dimmers and settle upon 3050- or 3000-degree lamps, think about the fact that 600W dimmers for incandescent lamps may be purchased for less than five dollars apiece. Think too of the fact that by "dimming-up" a lamp, even if you promptly raise it to full voltage, it will last longer because the filament was "hit" gradually. rather than being slammed with 120V by the flick of a switch. Lastly. think of the dramatic effects possible through the use of dimmers. Incidentally, remember that incandescent lamps "sing" during the dimming-up period, and you must wait a few moments for this very audible noise to subside.

The innovative "quartz" lamps are a form of the incandescent. The filament is tungsten in halogen which has as its most redeeming feature the ability to be free of flaking and darkening through nearly 100% of its life. The small size of the lamp is made possible by the quartz envelope that encases the filament and gas. Quartz is the only practical substance capable of withstanding the extreme temperature generated over a very small area. Quartz lamps should not be handled when hot as they are known to break when in this state. The advantages of all the tungsten-halogen designs are, in addition to small size and Kelvin-retention, long life and very high efficiency.

If you decide to invest in some "store bought" low-cost dimmer devices, bear in mind the following. They must often be derated if placed near each other, such as within a small housing. That is, two 600W electronic dimmers, side by side, should not feed more than 500W loads each. Many of these units closely grouped may require forced-air cooling. But worst of all, inexpensive triacs may generate rf radiation that will wreak havoc with your audio and your video. This noise will be radiated by the dimmers, the cables, and even the lamps. So, test two or three of the dimmers of your choice (*one* is not enough!), together, before you invest dollars and time in building your own dimmerboard.

However, if you want greater current-carrying capacity, remote control, scene presetting, scene mastering, "pile-on" (that's literally adding one set of presets to another, and is used extensively in the legitimate theatre), and the sophisticated features and circuitry of a specialized "little theatre" system, there are various units available at surprisingly low cost. The device shown in Fig. 13-2 offers all the foregoing features and a few more. Any circuit may be switched off the master so that it will not be faded with the group. It provides internally illuminated controls that are linear in motion for easy readout and operator convenience; unaltered tracking and repeatability of dimmer settings regardless of input line variations or wide changes in load. The filtering system virtually eliminates lamp-filament noise as well as radiation. The unit shown includes noise as well as radiation. The unit shown includes 12 2400W circuits with their respective 20A circuit breakers. You can buy a unit with half this capacity and retain the ability to have all circuits in each scene under the control of a single scene master.

## Putting It All Together in a Practical Studio

Bearing in mind all of the foregoing, we have effected a compromise in a studio we built that encompasses the three originally stated criteria—economy, efficiency, and versatility. First we decided that the color temperature we would shoot for was 3000° K. Next we realized that in most cases only the actors' faces necessitated careful color temp control. (If the *background colors* were "off," so what? No viewer would know that they weren't "exactly right.") Finally, because our soundstage was small and, like so many others, not professionally air conditioned, we used as many 500—600W fixtures as possible, relegating the "kilowatters" to cyclorama and background use—and that to be kept to a minimum.

The soundstage is 22 × 25 ft and is rigged to accommodate two separate sets (scenes), one about half the size of the other. The cameras turn 90 degrees to shoot one scene or the other. The lighting grid is shown in Fig. 13-3. All cables run along the pipes to two six-circuit plugboxes, only one of which is dimmable. Our assessment of overall economies weighed against flexibility dictated that if we dimmed half of our circuits, such would be sufficient. Every lamp and its cable is numbered so that we can decide if we wish to dim that lamp or not, then plug it into the appropriate dim or nondim system. The plugs are three-wire twist-locks, as the old-style stage plugs used in the theatre and in motion picture production are rapidly being superseded. The remote-control panel for the dimmerbank is operated from the audio-video control room during showtime, but is brought into the studio for setup—and may be operated in the studio at *any* time.

It is a well-proven rule in television, as in the legitimate theatre, that one should keep the lights off the floor. Contrary to motion picture production, where many floor-standing lights plus others on floor-standing platforms are utilized, there is too much hustle and bustle in the theatre and in television to permit floor-standing devices which are always in the way and are often quite hazardous. The closest we get to a floor luminaire is one that would be mounted on a camera—and this we avoid whenever possible. If you need a lamp lower than the others, use a pantograph. The pantograph we selected holds the light some 18 in. beneath the pipebatten when compressed; and can lower the light more than 12 ft in extended mode. Unfortunately, the "pant" is more expensive than any of the luminaires, but include at least one of these in your studio plans. We use 1¼ in. (I.D.) pipes and everything mounts to

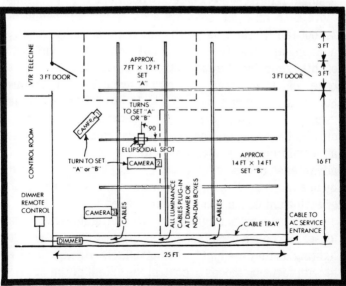

Fig. 13-3. Actual layout of a practical studio.

Fig. 13-4. High-intensity ellipsoidal spotlight serves as a key light or pattern projector for effects. (Courtesy Century-Strand.)

them via C-clamps. Figure 13-4 shows a Lekolite on the pipe via C-clamp. We use the built-in push-shutters, add a pattern holder and then are able to take advantage of the great intensity (efficiency) and controllability of the ellipsoidal-design spotlight as a pattern display or "key" light.

We have also been lucky enough to avail ourselves of a unique, incredibly efficient cyclorama illuminant of revolutionary design, created in Italy and now available in North America. Figure 13-5 shows a quadruple complex, but singles and doubles (vertical and horizontal) are available. A single Ianiro cyclite, correctly positioned, will illuminate more than an eight-foot-wide area of the full height of a 24-foot-tall cyclorama with no bottom light required, amazing as it may seem. And what's more, the construction of this luminaire eliminates the hard light line found at the base of most cycs lit by conventional luminaires. Substituting the relatively costly Ianiro for the customary "scoops," we actually *save* time and money because we use only half as many luminaires, pull less current, require less air conditioning, replace fewer lamps—besides having the advantages of a *pole light*. (*Every* adjustment is operable by one man standing on the floor and using only a pole, thus effecting untold man-hours in time saved.)

Our primary set-lighting is via spotlights with Fresnel lenses. So called open-face lenses are unsuitable for indoor lighting as they are highly uncontrollable. Backgrounds are lit with focusing scoops to control the extent of the flood, the latter using 1 kW lamps, whereas the spotlights are 500W

Fig. 13-5. Unusually efficient quadruple floodlight created especially for cyclorama usage. (Courtesy Century-Strand.)

because our studio is small and the ceiling low. Some spotlights are fitted with four-way barndoors to precisely control coverage and "spill," and every luminaire accepts a color frame. Our total is 12 6-in. Fresnel spotlights, one ellipsoidal, three cyclites, five scoops and the previously discussed six-circuit dimmer plus six nondim circuits in a 22 × 25 ft studio. This kind of demand requires a 100A, 240V single-phase electrical service.

Quartz lamps, in particular, must be handled with great care; otherwise you will break them or curtail their output and/or life. Never handle them when they are warm. Always grasp them at the base(s) only and if you *must* touch the body of the lamp, wear clean gloves, or clean the quartz with alcohol. Burnish the lamp contacts if necessary and at the time of relamping also burnish the socket contacts to eliminate arcing which is severely damaging, besides being annoying.

# Chapter 14

## Dealing With Acoustics Is Tricky—Here's How

If there were one piece of advice to give the videoman (or the audioman, for that matter) in the area of acoustical design it would be: *consult an expert*. Acoustical engineering is a highly specialized field, and building construction generally is a one-time and costly endeavor, so it is penny-wise and pound-foolish to leap into the acoustics arena, regardless of how many years you've spent in the electronics, or even the production end of the audio or video world.

However, with a knowledge of basic acoustics, you can do a great deal of preliminary studio layout work yourself, leaving only the (critical) fine points (construction rules and specifications) to the acoustician you hire. Rest assured, whatever you pay him will pay off.

To illustrate how crucial acoustic decisions are, you have only to look at the problems that plagued New York's Lincoln Center, where one of the most famous acousticians in the land ran into serious trouble. A new consultant was called in, and has made change after expensive change over a decade, with results that still do not satisfy many experts.

Then there's the famous Hollywood Bowl which even the Coast's most celebrated acoustician, the late Vern Knudsen of UCLA, couldn't save. Interestingly enough, the finest concert halls, acoustically—and that's what counts—are in Europe, designed by masters who were perhaps loathe to pass their secrets on. Now let's look at a few "open secrets."

Walk into most any recording studio and you'll see loads of fancy acoustic tile on walls and ceiling. This material serves two functions: (1) to dress up the walls; and (2) to absorb as much as possible of the sound hitting the walls. "What!" you exclaim, "absorb the sound?" That's right. Contrary to popular misconception, this top layer of smart-looking fiberboard which comes in various sizes, shapes, patterns, and now even colors (those rock 'n' rollers like things psychedelic) is there to "hold" the sound, and keep it from bouncing back into the room. Without this, the room would reverberate to an unbearable degree.

Even so, not all the sound will be absorbed so the phenomenon known as *standing waves* will be encountered, creating a very uneven pattern of sound in the room. These are in reality reflections that are in phase with original sound at certain frequencies. (The highly touted Capitol Records Hollywood studios had this problem with violins when the rooms were first built.)

To minimize the problem of standing waves the studio should have no parallel walls. This means the ceiling should not be parallel to the floor, either! If you must use a room whose walls and ceiling are already there, consider the design shown in Fig. 14-1, where we also see how the ceiling has been angled.

Wallboard is the ideal material for low-cost soundproofing. Its purpose is to not only realign wall and ceiling surfaces, but to also help prevent sound from passing through in either direction. A second essential part of studio acoustics is isolating the studio from external sound. Two main principles apply: heavy walls minimize the passage of sound; but they must be isolated to eliminate solid pathways into the studio from outside because sound travels well in solid materials. (See Fig. 14-2.)

Three layers of wallboard should suffice. Don't put identical thicknesses next to each other! This may cause sympathetic vibration. Don't nail them to each other or to the $2 \times 4$'s, glue them! Nails are solid pathways, and will transfer sound. Figure 14-2 shows this suggestion in detail. The wallboard will have absorbing material fastened to it (see detail).

The $2 \times 4$ in. studs (uprights) usually rest on another two-by-four that runs the length of the wall. The adjacent

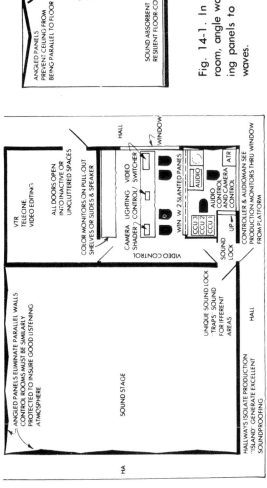

Fig. 14-1. In using an existing room, angle wall panels and ceiling panels to minimize standing waves.

LINED AIR CONDITIONING DUCT

BAFFLE

ANGLED PANELS PREVENT CEILING FROM BEING PARALLEL TO FLOOR

ONE METHOD OF WINDOW GLASS MOUNTING REDUCES LIGHT & SOUND REFLECTIONS

MIC STORAGE

AC OUTLETS

SOUND ABSORBENT RESILIENT FLOOR-COVERING

VTR TELECINE VIDEO EDITING

ALL DOORS OPEN INTO INACTIVE OR UNCLUTTERED SPACES

COLOR MONITORS ON PULL-OUT SHELVES OR SLIDES & SPEAKER

HALL

WINDOW

VIDEO CONTROL

CAMERA SHADER

LIGHTING CONTROL

VIDEO CONTROL/ SWITCHER

WIN. W 2 SLANTED PANES

AUDIO

SOUND LOCK

CCU 3
CCU 2
CCU 1

AUDIO CONTROL AND CAMERA CONTROL

ATR

SOUND UP

CONTROLLER & AUDIOMAN SEE PRODUCTION MONITORS THRU WINDOW FROM PLATFORM

ANGLED PANELS ELIMINATE PARALLEL WALLS CONTROL ROOMS MUST BE SIMILARLY PROTECTED TO INSURE GOOD LISTENING ATMOSPHERE.

UNIQUE "SOUND LOCK" "TRAPS" SOUND FOR DIFFERENT AREAS

HALL

SOUND STAGE

HALLWAYS ISOLATE PRODUCTION "ISLAND" GENERATE EXCELLENT SOUNDPROOFING

HA

wall will be built the same way. Be certain that the wood and wallboard of one wall does not touch that of another, forming a solid path from one room to the other. For the same reason, take care that only the sealant joins the corners!

Whenever possible, avoid having your studio use an outside wall adjacent to the street or shared by another tenant. And try to let as much of your soundstage as possible be next to an interior hallway. Halls are usually very quiet, thus you'll have little worry about noises getting in, or of your sounds bothering outsiders. So, if you have two soundstages, put a hallway between them.

Your acoustics specialist will tell you where to purchase special doors which are designed for maximum sound attenuation. Some doors are built on the principle of a huge slab of lead inside. Others take an opposite approach and go for a "floating" interior. One of the problems is that doors must open easily yet close tightly and furthermore must not rest on a sill which would impair moving heavy and delicate equipment in and out of the studio. There are some unique gadgets designed to raise automatically when a door is opened, yet provide a soft seal between the floor and the door when the latter is closed. They are obtainable through

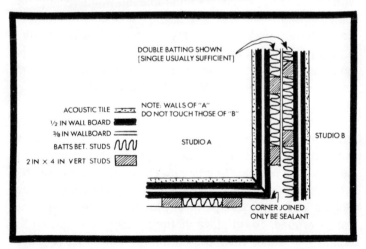

Fig. 14-2. Glue three layers of wallboard to studs and cover with acoustic tile.

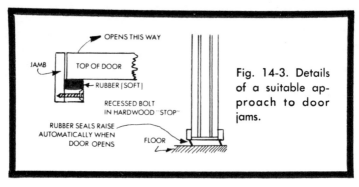

Fig. 14-3. Details of a suitable approach to door jams.

builder's supply and major hardware stores. Figure 14-3 details design of one type of door and jamb.

If I've said it once I've said it a thousand times: Eliminate the control room window! It is a throwback to radio broadcasting and recording studios—*you are in television*. Use an inexpensive TV camera with wide-angle lens to see into your studio, and save yourself the expense and headaches of acoustically treated windows which will be covered by drapes, sets, lights, people, equipment and props, anyway.

But one handy place for a window is between the control room and the hall. It's purpose is to let visitors see in without entering, especially an employee who's looking for someone and is not sure he's inside. At least two panes of glass are required, and not only must they not be parallel but they should not be the same thickness. One method of mounting glass that avoids the sound transfer and light reflection characteristics of parallel panes is that shown in Fig. 14-1.

Soundstages need not be designed to be as aesthetically attractive as recording studios. It is wasteful to affix *decorative* acoustic tile to the walls for absorption since there is little occasion to enjoy it. The ceiling is masked by lights and other rigging. The walls may be screened by weights and ropes and pulleys, plus all of the equipment that is around. So, in place of the acoustic tile needed to absorb the sound, video men often put rockwool or glass fiber blanketing in batts. This substance can be glued to the wallboard, then must be covered to prevent it harming people who rub against it. The covering can be burlap, which is thin, cheap and plentiful. Then the batting with the burlap draped over it is held in place by a grid of widely spaced steel wires, horizontal and/or vertical. Many times chicken wire is used for this purpose instead. Don't forget that your control room must be given the same amount of acoustic thought as your soundstage. The control room will probably demand acoustic tile finish to make it more presentable.

Lastly, we encounter the problem of air conditioning. Again, your acoustics consultant should be your guide. Of primary importance is slow motion of the air to minimize *air rush*. To help in this area, place a curved baffle a few inches from each of the outlets. Your acoustician will give you pointers on how to prevent the air ducts from carrying sound between studio and control room, and even other areas on the same system.

The conditioner's machinery is a major source of noise. It may require installation of baffles at each outlet plus thick noise-suppression pads at the junction between the machine and the ducts. Don't overlook the return-air (exhaust) ducting and its tendency to transfer and carry sound. All supply ducts should have cork linings, or may even require a few feet of fiberglass batts at each outlet. If heavy smokers are encountered you may have to install exhaust fans at the return-air outlets. Give careful attention to the amount of heat to be generated by your luminaires, for your air conditioner must accommodate this.

And whereas fluorescent fixtures make the most economical work lights, their ballasts are noisy, so be sure they're turned off during production. Keep microphones away from air ducts. Wiring ducts also create soundproofing hazards, sometimes carrying sound from one room to another. Conduits (even large ones) will minimize this possibility. But watch out for a conduit inadvertently becoming the rigid link between two rooms that "short circuits" your sound isolation and destroying your best-laid plans!

# Chapter 15

# Equipment Tips For Improved Production

It would seem appropriate here in this book on every major aspect of the low-cost color TV studio to discuss many of the factors relating to the production of a television show, whether it be for entertainment or instruction. In this way you may find it worthwhile to revise your thinking with respect to personnel, equipment selection, equipment placement, studio floor plans, etc.

If you've ever visited a commercial television studio—I strongly urge you to do so—you probably noted that when the monitors are not displaying a picture, their faces are black. Is this true with your monitors? When you "fade to black," are you really fading to "white"? If the white scan lines can be seen in the absence of a picture, your monitors are no doubt not equipped with *dc restoration*. This inexpensive circuit addition not only blanks the screen in the absence of video information, but you will be delighted to find that your blacks are blacker and your whites whiter.

Resetting of your brightness and contrast controls will be required. But here you reap yet another bonus from dc restoration. With the brightness reduced, the voltage bombarding the kinescope will be less, thus prolonging tube life. Furthermore, the contrast (video gain) control will have to be set higher, which often results in improvement of the low-frequency response. One word of caution with respect to use of dc restoration: If your monitor has no pilot light it is near-impossible to tell when the power is on because you see no scan lines on the blank screen. Secondly, certain monochrome monitors may develop high-voltage difficulties under dc restoration if left on for many hours without video information fed to them. Figure 15-1 shows one form of dc restoration.

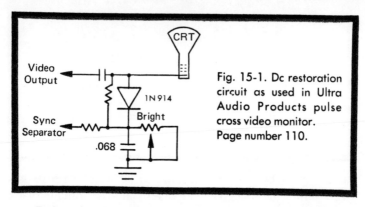

Fig. 15-1. Dc restoration circuit as used in Ultra Audio Products pulse cross video monitor. Page number 110.

Before leaving the matter of fades to black, there are other factors to consider. As pointed out earlier in a previous chapter, in color television when fading to black, you cannot just fade to nothing, you *must* fade to *something*, namely a source of black. In other words, black (as provided by a color-black generator) becomes one of the sources, just like a camera, fed to one of the inputs of your video switcher. Without this your fades would be to a very "noisy" screen with streaks and flashes throughout. Because a black-burst generator is costly, some people take an inexpensive monochrome camera, which could also be used for titling, and point it towards a dull black surface, then fade to this camera. Not ideal, but a good cost-saver, especially when one considers that small-production switchers accept only a limited number of inputs, usually five or six, one of which must be "lost" to the black-burst source.

There *is* a way to avoid tying up one of your precious input sources of the switcher in dedicating it to black. By connecting a two-input mini-fade mixer to the output of your switcher, then feeding the switcher's output to one input of the mini-fade and your black-burst generator to the other, your fades to black may be accomplished on *this* unit (see Fig. 15-2), and you will still have all of your switcher's inputs available for other sources. An AGC amplifier is a helpful production device for correcting operator errors in video levels, particularly important when operating with inexperienced crews. If you use one, be sure it is connected

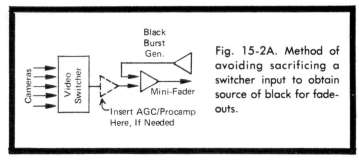

Fig. 15-2A. Method of avoiding sacrificing a switcher input to obtain source of black for fade-outs.

in the circuit before the mini-fader. Otherwise, the AGC unit will "hunt" for a video signal when you are fading to black and thus increase system noise unnecessarily in the absence of pictures.

### In the Multistudio

If you are fortunate enough to have a multistudio facility, some form of master control will be required when transferring *on the air* status from one studio to another—or even when switching from, say, studio to VTR . When accomplishing this switch, try to do so during the time when you are "in black." The reason is that you will undoubtedly

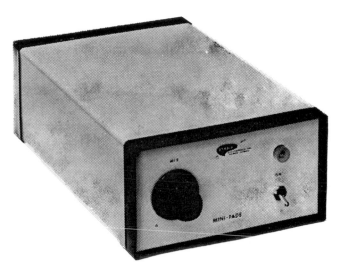

Fig. 15-2B. Two-input "outboard" video fader permits proper fades to black without sacrificing a video-switcher input. (Courtesy Dynair.)

be switching sync sources along with video, and all the receivers watching your program will lose sync temporarily. This same rule applies when you are going in and out of genlock, or when changing genlock sources. You will recall that genlock is that marvelous aspect of the better sync generators that permits them to synchronize to composite video from a video tape recorder, another studio, or from remote-program source. This allows you to "cut" from one composite source to another without losing the all-important sync stability.

But to do this you must preset your sync generator, via its genlock input, to synchronize to that other composite source for later program-switching convenience. Because there will be sync instability during the generator lockup time, the genlock must also be accomplished while in black. It should be pointed out that you cannot expect to effect your genlock to a VTR playback unless the tape is in motion (the sync pulses are on it) and the VTR's output is feeding the sync-generator's genlock input (even if you haven't yet switched the tape's program on the air yet).

Have you given any thought to failure of your sync generator? The cost of a sync generator could easily amount to less than 2%, perhaps even as little as 1%, of your total equipment investment; yet without it you're "down and out"! If you can afford one sync generator, you *cannot* afford not to have two. Obviously, sync must fail while the system is in use, at which time pandemonium will ensue. To prevent this, accompany your backup (standby) sync generator with a manual (or more costly automatic) sync-changeover device which instantly indicates a failure in any of your primary sync generator's outputs and effects immediate changeover to your standby unit. The downtime will then be only a few seconds, at most. Inasmuch as you'll be using a number of pulse-distribution amplifiers and probably a few video DA's, use plug-in types because not only do they take up less space, but you can pull one and push in a spare far quicker than running around the rack and locating and changing over as many as five or more cables—while production staff and actors hover over you making you a nervous wreck.

You may wish to utilize camera monitors equipped with underscan. This allows you to see what appears in the corners and all edges of your television picture—areas normally hidden on home receivers and even on studio monitors. If you forego this aspect in your camera monitors, why not at least provide it in your program-line and preview monitors, one of which should also have pulse cross display capability. (This will be discussed in the next chapter.)

# Chapter 16
# People and Equipment:
# The Proper Combination
# Is a Must

How big a technical crew you will need depends upon the type and complexity of your equipment and productions. A tabletop outfit with one or two cameras might require only one or two crew members, each performing multiple tasks—camera work, lighting, shading, switching, audio and VTR operation. But for other than the most modest activities, you will have to enlist the services of a number of persons.

It is not necessary that they be engineers or even technicians, but they will require eagerness, devotion and a knowledge of television practices, habits, and terminology; otherwise your productions will be needlessly time-consuming, laborious and amateurish—while you compete with "Hollywood's best" for the viewer's attention, whether you like it or not.

A sophisticated three-camera color studio should utilize the talents of a shader, a cameraman on each live camera, an audioman, Telecine/VTR operator, lighting man (the VTR operator or the shader might serve double-duty here), and a director.

The director is not necessarily a part of the technical staff. If the technical director, in this case the switcher operator, has artistic capabilities, and if the production is not too elaborate or intricate artistically, the TD could also function as the show director. You might also utilize a floor manager to cue the actors.

The shader is the person who "rides gain" on the cameras. Prior to show time he works with the cameramen in optimizing and matching camera outputs. In addition to the camera-picture monitors, the shader relies upon two other tools, one of which is the waveform monitor — the

Fig. 16-1. Internal-calibrating voltage displayed against graticule calibrated in IRE units. (Courtesy United Audio Pixtec.)

television equivalent of audio's VU meter. The introduction of low-cost WFMs makes possible the use of one on each and every camera's output, whereas prior to their availability it was necessary to switch one expensive WFM from camera to camera in a vain attempt to accomplish the job, or to leave the unit connected to the program line and hope to "clean up" the cameras after they're switched "on the air," which obviously is too late.

Close study of the waveform monitor's graticule reveals that it is calibrated in IRE units from 0 to 100 and 0 down to -40, the latter being the sync area. After the shader has calibrated the WFM per manufacturer's instructions, he makes certain there are 40 IRE units of sync and then sets camera pedestal. This is the point of "jet black" in the picture. The graticule has a special line at 7.5 IRE, and black level is set at this point or as much as (but no higher than) 10 IRE units. The brightest picture portion permissible is 100 IRE units.

### Don't Rely On Meters

Output-level meters (furnished with some cameras) are unreliable for many reasons: (1) they indicate average rather than peak video levels, (2) they are slow acting. (3) they do not display the intensities of the individual portions of the scene.

This latter item is one of the major advantages of the waveform monitor, especially inasmuch as it is an excellent double check on scene lighting quality. The WFM displays two lines of video, thus permitting the shader to see the horizontal blanking between lines. The full aspects of the WFM have either been discussed in prior chapters of this book or will be elaborated upon in later discussions of equipment maintenance.

The second device of importance to the shader during setup is a camera chart. More than any other tool, this accessory makes camera matching a reality. It would be ideal if such a chart could be focused upon under actual set (scene) lighting conditions. If the shader is concerned about a certain camera's setup during a show, the camera can be effortlessly turned towards the setup chart which can be located slightly out of camera range, but still under the scene lighting in use, and recalibrated quickly. The camera manufacturer's setup procedures are then followed.

Most production switchers incorporate a few of the most preferred special effects, usually various kinds of "wipes" in addition to the "dissolve." You will want to use a switcher that offers "preview" capability so that you will know what your effect will look like before you put it on the air. Hopefully you will also be able to feed the proposed effect to the viewfinder of the camera that is to be used to accomplish this effect. This aids the cameraman in positioning his camera quickly. Without this extra circuitry, the cameraman must rely solely upon positioning instructions from the director, which is often time consuming.

One of the most popular bits of electronic trickery is the matte shot in which a subject is keyed into a background located elsewhere. Used in motion picture filming for years, it is much easier to do in television.

Video switchers equipped with a key-effect capability allow you to insert an object taken by a camera on the

Fig. 16-2A. Subject in front of blue background seen by camera on video switcher's B-bus, to be keyed into A-bus.

switcher's B-bus (usually) into a background being photographed by another camera connected to the A-bus. A has the keyhole into which you'll insert the picture from B. But if the A background is to be used in the completed picture, how do you get rid of the background which is presently a part of the B picture? The answer is what is known as *chroma key*.

We are all indebted to Bob Pierce for this fabulous creation. The chroma key relies upon the fact that a color camera's encoder offers separate red, green, and blue outputs in addition to the encoded, vectored NTSC output. Now, if you were to place a person in front of a blue background, and if you then used only the red and green camera outputs, the blue background would not be there. You then could key that person into any other background (setting).

You may select any of the three primary colors as the chroma-key color. Green is sometimes used, but blue is preferred because it is a weak color. Of course the subject being keyed must not wear blue, and should avoid wearing

Fig. 16-2B. Background seen by camera on switcher's A-bus.

clothes whose colors incorporate blue (cyan or purple for example). Furthermore, if the key subject has blue eyes, don't use a closeup or you'll find only black voids where the eyes should be.

Chroma key is used extensively in television news shows to insert the newscaster into the background (usually a film of a news happening). Bad chroma key or bad lighting of the key subject will result in a blue or green fringe around him during the keying sequence. Chroma key is also effective on live comedy or variety shows. It is now possible to chroma-key a composite NTSC signal (such as videotape) into another background, although the cost of such keying device is high. Figure 16-2 A, B, C illustrates the use of chroma key.

### Burst Inhibit

If your programming entails running amounts of monochrome pictures, such as motion picture film, you must provide for *burst inhibit*. The FCC,which is far more adamant about (all) pulses than about pix, requires that color subcarrier not be present during purely monochrome sequences. Among other things, this is to prevent spurious color from being present in the black and white pictures.

There are devices that will sense monochrome and inhibit the subcarrier automatically; or you may do so

Fig. 16-2C. Matte shot with B subject keyed in A background via chroma key.

manually. There are also devices which act upon sources that are "fuzzy" compared to the live camera's sharp output. These are known as *image enhancers*. Most film and some videotape require varying amounts of crispening. The image enhancer can even be automatic to detect moments of reduced resolution and insert the necessary amount of enhancement. If you plan to run much film or helical videotape, an image enhancer is a most worthwhile adjunct.

### Other "Lifesavers"

Other aids to good teleproduction are a prompting device for speakers, or even to cue actors, that is motor-driven and incorporates the script on a wide paper roll; and a surveillance camera permitting the control-room staff to have an overall view of the soundstage to see where everything and everyone is located. This is much more effective and less expensive than control-room windows which also are hard to soundproof and are usually blocked by personnel, equipment, and sets.

In addition to a complement of tools, have on hand various pieces of dull black cloth for covering reflective objects on remotes, single-face and double-face sticky tape, electrical tape, cube taps, short extension cords, three-wire to two-wire adapters, flashlights, ac voltmeter (you'd be amazed at how low the power voltage is at certain remote locations), VTR-head cleaner and associated accessories, push-pins, nails with protruding heads for easy removal, tape measure, chalk, motion picture-style clapstick/slate for identification of productions and "takes," battery-powered "bullhorn" or megaphone, and a portable ac trouble light. Operating experience will no doubt reveal the need for various other "lifesavers."

# Chapter 17

## The Hell With Helicals

Unquestionably the most talked about technical topic in the area of program origination for CATV is that of the problems inherent to the use of low-cost studio equipment—particularly inexpensive helical-scan video tape recorders, reel-to-reel and cassette. So intense is this situation that the NCTA, under Engineering Vice-President Delmer Ports, is conducting a continuing study of the helical VTR with respect to standardization, tape interchangeability, picture and sync quality, reliability, and maintenance.

The CATV operator faces a presently insurmountable dilemma. His programming originations must compete with lavishly produced shows prepared on the most costly equipment using the most expensive artistic and production talent—and seen side by side with his own efforts on his own cable. If this weren't enough of a headache, he must soon face up to the fact that inasmuch as he is already under FCC jurisdiction, it is only a matter of time before the Commission is going to impose minimum technical standards. In the case of television, the FCC, in its "infinite wisdom," has always devoted its primary emphasis to the matter of synchronizing pulses rather than picture quality. Sync is *objective* while pix are *subjective*—to say nothing of the differences between color monitors, plus the people that watch them.

As a result of the introduction of integrated circuits, the cost of a broadcast-grade (EIA RS-170 sync plus NTSC color reference) synchronizing pulse generator is now so low that the cableman, in particular, should find it hard to justify the purchase of lesser-quality equipment, since there is a requirement for this to be, by force of circumstances, a cut above the in-house industrial TV producer in that his programming competes with commercial entertainment productions. Thus no longer is the master sync generator an unavoidable weak link in the studio system—the helical scan VTR now stands alone in this area.

### The VTR: Source of Problems

What's wrong with today's helicals? When the first professional audio tape recorder was introduced in the United States it ran at a speed of 30 inches per second. Later, with improvements in tape, drive systems, and heads, professional speed was reduced to 15 ips for recording studios and 7.5 ips for radio stations (especially inasmuch as the bandwidth of broadcast-grade tape recorders at even this speed exceeds that of all AM radio transmitters). Interestingly, the 16- and 24-track tape recorders being sold to recording studios today no longer offer 7.5 and 15 ips speeds but instead are set for 15 and 30. Doesn't all this tell you something? Yet no helical video tape recorder has ever run at more than 7.5 ips, and most U.S.-made machines run considerably slower. If tape motion (wow, flutter, and timing) is a problem in professional audio, it only stands to reason that it is a greater problem in video. This condition is further aggravated by the video-head wheel instabilities not found in audio.

An insurmountable surfeit of problems, you say? To a certain extent, yes. But if you are willing to deliver good sync to your VTR and if you are willing to spend as much (or more) on your VTR and its accessories as you spent on your color camera (that's a good rule of thumb, by the way), there is hope. And, to my way of thinking, the FCC, coupled with the forces of competition, will compel this sooner or later, whether you like it or not. Is this "unfair?" Definitely not, when you consider that thousands of television receivers may be trying to lock to the sync pulses your helical-scan recorder is feeding them. In fact, your responsibility is awesome. Think about it—before you buy that cassette recorder with the picture that looks so good.

Fig. 17-1. A sophisticated video processor with various plug-in modules will correct most slant-track difficulties. (Courtesy 3M Co.)

Think too, that a tape you received from somewhere else—even a dub made under absolutely ideal conditions—will have about eight times the motion and tracking problems than when the master tape was originally made!

**Processors Help**

To minimize this situation a number of manufacturers have introduced helical-scan processors of varying degrees of sophistication, one of the most elaborate of which is shown in Fig. 17-1. It offers dropout compensation, sync and pix processing, sync regeneration, and video and chroma AGC, some of the foregoing being optional accessories. Let's see what this unit does. Recognizing that dropouts (momentary losses of picture created by brief reductions in rf carrier amplitude caused by tape surface irregularities or dirt on the tape or heads) are a source of concern in broadcast-grade quadruplex recorders and thus even more problematical in helicals, 3M-Mincom has incorporated a DOC feature in its processor. This circuit is connected by user to the rf output *inside* his helical VTR. Simple instructions permitting one to do this with any standard-made helical recorder are provided. This "trick" is the secret by which the dropout compensator is able to sense the intermittent loss of carrier. When this happens the one-line delay system in the DOC is electronically switched in and furnishes a repeat of the previous video line stored therein.

As long as there are no dropouts, nondelayed video is delivered by the DOC. If there is a loss, the DOC delivers the previous line signal. Due to similarity between successive

122

video lines, the viewer is not made aware of the substituted material. A word of caution: Since the DOC is sensitive to loss of rf rather than video, it cannot compensate for recorded-in dropouts. Thus if you are playing a dub containing dropouts made when the dub was made, this would reproduce as a loss of video, about which the dropout compensator can do nothing. The DOC will, however, provide compensation for new dropouts created *in playback* of the dub—or any tape. If it is not already apparent to the reader, these helical *procdocs* are used only in tape playback; other types of processors may be used on the program line during recording, and are used to clean up the line, not the tape.

The video and sync processor included in our example-product here, receives the regular output of the helical tape recorder. This is where we begin to correct the many sync irregularities, created by machine and tape alike, about which we have been speaking. Video processing encompasses many areas, and this device attacks them all—hum, tilt (poor low-frequency response), improper video levels, poor or even nonstandard sync, and finally the noise and disruptions caused during the head crossover, the latter being the principal cause of the difficulty or inability to dub from helical tape to quadruplex or motion picture film.

Our processor clamps the incoming signal on the incoming signal on the "back porch" to remove large amounts of hum or low-frequency bounce. The sync portion of the composite source is stripped off and used to lock the PROCAMPS own oscillator which then generates its own horizontal and vertical sync in exact phase with incoming sync signal. Clean sync and blanking, correctly RS-170 specification-timed, is inserted; the color burst is also gated out, amplified, limited, reshaped, and reinserted.

Figure 17-2A shows a pulse cross display of jitter created by probably the worst possible condition encountered—bad tracking. Coupled with noise spikes generated when each head-switch occurs, the TV monitor or receiver's AFC is hard put to deliver a stable picture

Fig. 17-2A. A pulse cross monitor reveals noise, sync disruptions, and transients during vertical interval. (Courtesy Ultra Audio Products.)

Fig. 17-2B. Same tape as shown in Fig. 17-2A after processing has restored all aspects of sync pulses (but no time-base correction). (Courtesy Ultra Audio Products.)

display. This processor resolves that condition by automatically switching to an internal 31.5 kHz oscillator during the head-crossover period using an AFC designed especially for the tension errors typical of the helical VTRs. An adjustment is provided to set this "lockout window" to the amount of time required by each individual video tape recorder. The result of this processing is shown by the superb sync displayed in Fig. 17-2B. Similarly, Figs. 17-3A and 17-3B show a waveform monitor expanded display of the vertical interval head-crossover period before and after processing, respectively. The stability improvements through processing are immediately apparent, even to the casual observer.

## But Time Base Correction Is Not Easy

The user who invests in a slant-track processor and gets a pulse cross display as good as that of Fig. 17-2B may be tempted to sit back smugly, content that his troubles are over. Regrettably, they are not. Because even the best of processors does not include one crucial, and terribly costly, aspect—time base correction. All of the instabilities of the machine's transport mechanism, added to the problem created by magnetic tape shrinkage and stretch, combine to generate sync-pulse time-base variations of usually immense magnitude. "But," you say, "I'm using a fine processor; the pulse cross display is rock-steady; and the sync-pulse edges are sharp and noise is reduced to near-nothing!" The problem, however, is that the pulse cross monitor is too "forgiving" to display even aggravated time-base errors. The instability is there but the pulse cross monitor is not sensitive enough to show it.

Thus we naturally arrive at the logical question, "If a precision studio monitor cannot display time-base error, and if the picture is steady in the normal display mode, why do I need time-base correction or sync processing at all?" This question is particularly poignant for the cableman who is currently putting cassettes on the line and is receiving no bad reaction from his customers. The Sony U-Matic has been viewed with keen interest by cable operators since

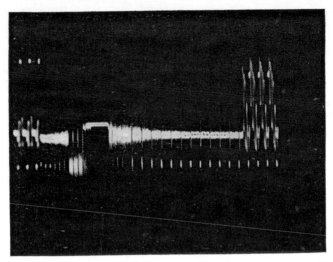

Fig. 17-3A. Expanded display on waveform monitor of vertical interval indicating serious noise and sync distortions prior to any playback processing. (Courtesy 3M Co.)

tape tension variation is less than that encountered with reel-to-reel units. Perhaps part of the answer lies in the fact that the customer may be as forgiving as his monitors. The viewer who watches a locally originated tape may be content to overlook the flagging at the top of the screen, the occasional picture leap, the periodic horizontal tearing, the *moire*, the poor color fidelity, and the full loss of color from time to time. But when the novelty wears off, will he be so tolerant?

The time-base correctors that are appearing on the market may be a solution for some operators albeit an expensive one. But even then, a $9000-unit may do you no good if your machine is not within a range that can be corrected. Which time-base errors can be corrected, and what time-base correctors can and can't do for you is the subject of a future book.

### A Few Other Points To Worry About

Bear in mind, if the tape you play is a second generation dub, you run the great risk that the heretofore minimal problems will suddenly achieve epic proportions. Rest assured, the FCC is thinking about this and there is no

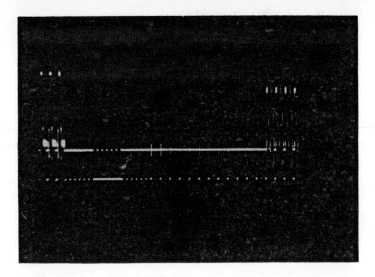

Fig. 17-3B. Processor creates clean and quiet sync in troublesome vertical-interval of head switching in slant-track tape playback. (Courtesy 3M Co.)

reason to believe that the cableman will ultimately be able to enjoy regulations less stringent than those imposed on his fellow broadcasters. (If the FCC doesn't, competition will see to that.)

This is not all. As 3M Company's project engineer Dick Fererro points out, how many helical VTRs have *any* method of controlling luminance or chrominance on tape playback? Are the tapes you make and the tapes you receive from outside sources so perfect that they require no attention? Very doubtful! Fortunately, the helical *procdoc* is the device that corrects not only these tapes but many of the deficiencies in the machines that play them. Your investment in a procdoc will compensate for a multitude of sins—head crossover noise, sloppy sync edges, improper luminance to chrominance relationships, flagging, color phasing, tension, dropouts, low video levels, high video levels, loss of sync, tape irregularities, hum, noisy recordings, and poor low-frequency response.

An appreciation of the seriousness of the helical situation can be gained by recognizing the problems still plaguing quadruplex users. I recently saw a quadruplex tape made at a network facility and played on another VTR in the same room. The playback machine was not equipped with velocity compensation and the result was a picture imperfect in various respects. Previously, I had seen a quad tape made in Puerto Rico, which traveled from the humid Caribbean to the temperate California climate, and played flawlessly in Hollywood. With this unpredictability in tapes made for use with hundred-thousand-dollar machines, how can the slant-track user expect to exist unaided with inexpensive gear? If the cableman plans to compete with the commercial broadcaster, either by design or by force of circumstances, he must face up to the idea of cleaning up or getting "cleaned out."

# Chapter 18

# Signal Monitor

If he hasn't already done so, the CATV operator must soon face up to the fact that programs he originates must come close in content, production value, and technical quality to those he retransmits upon their receipt from commercial TV stations. The viewer used to watching a slick, Hollywood-produced show is just not going to make allowances for a cableman's amateurish creations, further reduced to the point of pathetic humor by improper video levels coupled with abominable sync pulses emanating from helical-scan video tape recorders.

"But," you say, "I've got a meter on my VTR and I watch the video levels as much as humanly possible." Well, let's put it this way—a meter is much better than nothing. Unfortunately, meters have major and often misleading drawbacks. First of all, in the case of color, they cannot help you when the luminance and chrominance relationships change. When do they change? On inexpensive VTRs, for one thing, they alter every time you change the video-gain control's setting. Secondly, the meter is an averaging device (besides being slow-acting) in a circuit that demands peak-to-peak indications). Finally, the meter is unable to show you the light levels in the various portions of the scene being telecast. This is its most unfortunate attribute.

## How to Get True Readings

To remedy this we use a waveform monitor (WFM)—an oscilloscope whose sweep is synchronized to the TV-line rate (and which usually also can display at the TV-field rate, although this is used less frequently), and with intensity vertical. When set to read TV LINES, what lines does it display? All of them—but at the horizontal scan rate

Fig. 18-1. Waveform monitor displaying ten shades of gray at two TV lines rate.

(actually at half the line rate). Figure 18-1 shows an inexpensive waveform monitor receiving signals from a camera which is focused on a gray-scale card on which are printed ten vertical stripes, each ten percent different in shading intensity from the adjacent stripes. On the left is jet black, while the stripe farthest to the right is pure white. This produces a staircase pattern on the WFM, the foot of which is the black area on the left and the head being the white area on the right-handed portion of the card being televised.

Thus the waveform monitor shows us clearly the intensity or degree of brightness (illumination) in every individual portion of the picture, from left to right. Top to bottom intensity differences are expressed by a "bunching-up" of the monitor's scan lines wherever brightness is greater. In fact, this gives the appearance that the monitor's trace is brighter in these brighter picture portions.

The monitor's graticule (scale) is calibrated in IRE units (now called IEEE units); the base line being "0," the top line is "100." No portion of the scene's brightness should exceed, except momentarily, the 100-IRE point. If small areas of the scene exceed 100-IRE a meter would never catch it; in fact, the meter *always* reads too low, and you could be constantly overmodulating without ever knowing it.

Below the base line is a 40-unit section in 10-unit increments. This displays the sync portion of your video signal. Use this to make certain you have adequate sync strength—for sync is more crucial than pictures in broadcast and cable television (as the FCC rules will attest). Note the extra line on the graticule marked "7.5." This is known as the *setup* or *pedestal* level. If your cameras have pedestal controls, they should be adjusted for a 7.5 reading and, in this manner, the darkest portions of the picture will be at the 10-IRE (black) level, and readings lower than 10 will be "blacker than black."

**Using a Two-Line Display Also Shows Blanking**

The purpose of displaying two lines rather than one is to give adequate presentation of the horizontal blanking area, including the "back porch" area coming out of the picture and going into the horizontal blanking area, and the "front porch" portion after horizontal blanking and just before going into color burst or picture (if monochrome). The Ultra Audio WFM shown includes a control permitting you to spread the scan horizontally for detailed study of any portion of the video or sync signals.

The Ultra Audio WFM also includes a 1 volt internally generated source for the daily calibration. With this displayed on the screen the height of the trace is adjusted so that the bottom of the pattern is behind the − 40-IRE line and the top is behind the 100-IRE line. The WFM is then switched back to indicate program or camera output and will give accurate readings. Don't overlook the fact that the calibration voltage itself may change with age and probably should be compared with a known source of pure 1 volt ac peak-to-peak (not rms). Then any 1 volt source (camera reading a test chart, staircase generator, color bars or

Fig. 18-2. Pulse cross used to display vertical equalizing pulses on horizontal line; dark vertical line is horizontal blanking. Monitor can be switched to normal display. (Courtesy United Audio Pixtec.)

multiburst), as read on your calibrated WFM, may be fed to your VTR whose video-level meter should indicate in the proper area as shown on the meter's scale when the recorder's video-gain control has been set properly.

### Pulse Cross Display: A Must for VTRs

While helical VTRs are capable of giving excellent picture quality, the sync pulses they "lay down" on the tape are atrocious in ½-in. equipment and still generally unsatisfactory in 1-in. VTRs. The primary cause of this instability is the helical scan system itself coupled with tape motion irregularities as a consequence of inexpensive transport mechanisms. Before we can do anything to minimize this we must first *see* the synchronizing pulses. The pulse cross picture monitor makes this possible, and these are standard equipment on all quadruplex VTRs sold today. Figure 18-2 shows our same staircase pattern in a pulse cross display. Vertical equalizing pulses are shown in the right-hand horizontal arm of the cross. The horizontal blanking is the very dark vertical bar. If our signal were in color, a portion of this vertical bar would be a herringbone pattern representing the color burst that must appear at the start of every horizontal scan line of the picture.

Once we are able to see these sync pulses we can then adjust whatever controls are available on the VTR, such as skew, tracking, and tape tension, to minimize jitters seen in the display. Adjust controls so that variations, such as displayed on the pulse cross, are at the minimum possible. Your equipment will then be playing tape to the best of its ability.

**VITS May Also Be Seen**

A pulse cross monitor can be used anywhere in the video system. In fact, when connected to the output of a television demodulator you will be able to see in the lower horizontal lines of the blanking area whether the TV station you are receiving is transmitting Vertical Interval Test Signals on lines 17, 18, 19, or 20. Then, if you have a waveform monitor equipped to display them, you can give these important test signals considerable study at any point in a cable transmission system. Meanwhile, the pulse cross monitor allows continual surveillance of the sync, blanking, and equalizing pulses so that you may ascertain their stability.

# Chapter 19

# The Care and Feeding of Your VTR and Videotape

It is truly remarkable how well tabletop VTRs perform in view of the bouncing around they get as portables and the general lack of attention given them. They seem to "make pictures" in spite of the general neglect they receive. Nonetheless, a little thought plus a few moments of your time will reduce even further your chances of disappointment and possible financial loss. First, let's consider the protection your tapes need, both on and off of the machine.

Although it may not seem that way, videotape is subjected to momentary high temperature as a result of the pressure from the rotating video heads. Tape must have a high stability so that the loss of oxide during the abrasion process of recording or playback is minimal. Abrasion will diminish the depth of the oxide—ultimately to a point where the tape will no longer be usable. Unfortunately, loose oxide particles end up clogging all heads and adding to further wear. Therefore, clean all heads prior to each pass of the tape. This means stationary heads (erase, audio, and control track) as well.

Put no undue pressure on the rotating heads when cleaning, nor on the stationary ones, as alignment is critical, especially with the narrow track widths we must contend with. Do not place a tape on the VTR until the heads and the guides you've just cleaned are totally dry. This precaution is necessary because certain cleaning solvents should not be used: M.E.K., heptane, acetone, trichloroethylene, naptha, and xylene. Each of these chemicals displays one or more of the following undesirable characteristics: Softens or breaks down videotape; is flammable; swells rubber (the idlers); or is a health

Fig. 19-1. A winder reduces tape and head wear, makes a faster, better wind, and immediately frees VTR for other uses. (Courtesy United Audio Pixtec.)

hazard. Carbon tetrachloride is excellent and popular but its fumes constitute a health hazard in continued use. Freon TF is undoubtedly the best all-around solvent, but it's expensive. Probably the best buy is ethyl alcohol, and it should be obtainable in nonflammable form. VTR operators should not eat or smoke near the machine as invisible crumbs and smoke are major tape contaminants.

A serious problem with respect to tape life and picture/sync quality is created during tape rewind. Here, due to the absence of tape lifters such as those common on professional audio machines, the tape is compelled to be scraped at high speed against all stationary and rotating heads. This action abrades both tape and heads, needlessly shortening their lives and possibly diminishing low-frequency response of the tape and high-frequency response of the heads.

Figure 19-1 shows an inexpensive accessory rewinder created to eliminate this problem. The "Autowinder" also offers other benefits. It rewinds the tape at the correct tension. Tape wound too tightly may cause printthrough and binding, and tape wound too loosely (common on inexpensive video tape recorders) may cinch under temperature change and may also wind unevenly with the protruding edges, containing important audio and control-track information, subject to curling and edge damage.

Other advantages of the "Autowinder" are that it rewinds an hour's EIAJ tape in about a minute; it shuts off automatically whereas most of these VTRs will require manual resetting of the lever upon completion of the rewind; and rather than tying the VTR up for six to ten minutes of rewind, it frees the machine for immediate other usage.

After rewind (and at all times for that matter) be sure to store your tapes vertically, as an additional precaution against edge-damage, and preferably in a room offering 40%−45% relative humidity at 20°C (68°−69°F) temperature. This atmosphere also is conducive to maximum head life. Other temperatures and humidities will dramatically diminish head life—even as much as 50%.

There are many other, more sophisticated, preventive-maintenance procedures to follow. Most low-priced helicals use sliprings to transfer the rf signal to the spinning, video heads. These must be religiously cleaned while great care is exercised to avoid bending the wiper fingers. Dirty sliprings will ultimately lead to picture and/or sync breakup. If your VTR permits user balancing of the demodulators, do so occasionally by observing the bottom of the sync pulses and adjusting for minimum rf signal remaining on the video signals.

As you know, audio recorders superimpose the program signal on a high-frequency, high-level ac bias voltage. This is impractical for video because the bias oscillator would have to be extremely stable at an incredibly high frequency, such as 20 MHz or more. Consequently the video is instead modulated via double-sideband frequency modulation. The modulator's frequency deviations should be checked to insure that peak-white, sync tips, and black-level all occur at the frequencies recommended by the VTR manufacturer. This can be done by connecting a stable rf oscillator (while an appropriate test signal is applied to the VTR's output) and tuning the oscillator to the required frequency (as per manufacturer's specifications). A zero beat should occur on the demod's input when you've selected the specified frequency for each of the three aforementioned parameters (levels). If this is not the case, repair or adjustment may be in order.

Most color video tape recorders may be switched to record in monochrome. In the monochrome mode, you should feed ten-step staircase pattern into the machine and set the video-level pointer to the zero mark on the meter. Since these meters are highly inaccurate for other than reading a sustained video signal, a waveform monitor (Fig. 19-2) which is the video equivalent of the VU meter used in audio, should be used for all program-level indications. For recording in the color mode, it seems as though most EIAJ machines "like" to have the video level set (with standard color bars) just below the zero mark. This results in better color rendition most of the time. Then continue to use your waveform monitor for program monitoring at full level on the WFM.

Tip projection (of the video heads) is our final, but not least, concern. Insufficient projection will result in picture dropouts and a reduced signal-to-noise ratio. Too great projection will distort and thus damage the tape irreparably. Thus, tip projection must begin per manufacturer's specifications and be checked periodically to ascertain whether it has fallen below acceptability. You may also wish to assure yourself that the servomechanism is functioning properly. A quick check may be made by

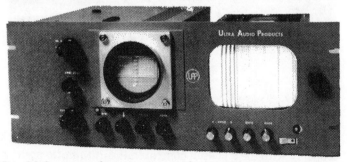

Fig. 19-2. A waveform monitor (with companion picture monitor, right) gives accurate level indications unobtainable on meters. Low-cost units available. (Courtesy United Audio Pixtec.)

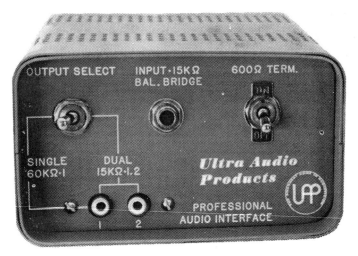

**A**

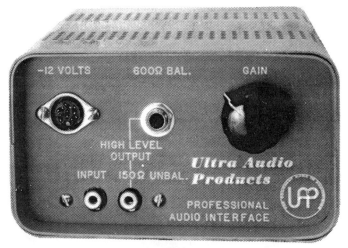

**B**

Fig. 19-3. Audio interfaces permit proper connection to other sources and leads, overcoming drawbacks of EIAJ VTRs.

playing a tape made on the same VTR. It should track properly with the tracking control in the *automatic* position and also when it is approximately in the center of the manually variable settings. If you are unable to obtain proper tracking thusly, your VTR may require repair. One of the disappointing aspects of most EIAJ-type VTRs is the low (usually about 0.1V across 500Ω) audio output. This is unsuitable for feeding many mixer amplifiers or other VTRs for dubbing. The product shown in Fig. 19-3 not only boosts the level to +8 dBm but also provides a 600Ω *balanced* output (which may be unbalanced by the user), thus rendering your VTR's audio to broadcast standards. You can then feed as much other equipment as desired. Another useful device is also shown. It makes possible the bridging connection of professional high-level balanced program lines to the unbalanced high impedance inputs of one or even two tabletop VTRs while maintaining isolative protection of the program line. Thus these two interface devices not only increase your recorder's versatility, but reduce operator tension and frustration as well when the studio is hectic and busy with production.

# Chapter 20

# *Maintenance & Calibration of the Low-Cost Color Teleproduction Center*

Has it occurred to you that most people have no idea how to set the *brightness, contrast, color intensity* and *hue* of their television receivers? (Do you know—for sure?) With test equipment every cable operator should possess (and every sophisticated CCTV colorcaster, too), the CATV system can make possible the calibration of every subscriber's receiver. Not only will this provide the obvious benefits of greater television enjoyment, but it will reduce complaints of "poor picture" from subscribers.

Why not transmit on a spare channel, or on your origination channel, a half hour (for example) of test signals to permit subscribers to set up their receivers? These transmissions could take place at say, 9 a.m. and 9 p.m. daily. They might consist of a ten-step staircase followed by NTSC color bars alternating in five-minute increments for a half hour. Superimposed over the step pattern for the first minute segment might be a "billboard" as shown in Fig. 20-1. For the first minute of each five-minute color-bar transmission, you might superimpose the description shown in Fig. 20-2.

"But these test generators are expensive!" you cry. Well, if you're a cable operator doing program origination, surely you'll want to calibrate your *own* studio monitors—unless you want to look as bad as possible in comparison to the commercial stations you carry. Believe it or not, monochrome monitors are used for the bulk of camera setup work, and they must be calibrated before you set up your color cameras. Then, your (calibrated) color monitor is used for precise camera-matching comparisons. In most instances you needn't purchase a color-bar

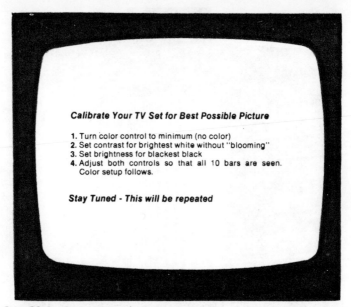

Fig. 20-1. Superimposed viewer instructions over first minute of staircase-pattern transmission to help subscriber set his receiver luminance.

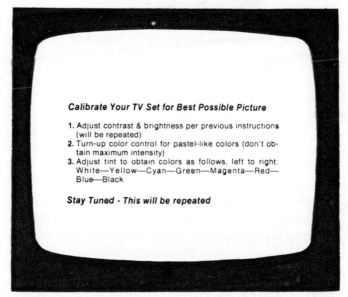

Fig. 20-2. Superimposed viewer instructions over first minutes of color-bar pattern transmission to set receiver chrominance.

Fig. 20-3A. Multiburst test signal gives quick check on system's high-frequency response. (Courtesy Ultra Audio Products.)

generator because your camera's encoder already contains one.

Your local newspaper should be only too glad to mention in each daily or weekly TV-program listing the service that you offer your televiewers. It goes without saying that you will find it worthwhile to transmit these patterns, along with multiburst, throughout the day to test system quality at whatever points your technicians require. Multiburst is a beautiful quick-check on your studio's and transmission-system's frequency response, the pattern displayed being that in Fig. 20-3A. The burst pattern usually consists of a white flag followed by short duration oscillations at 0.5 MHz, 1.25 MHz, 2 MHz, 3 MHz, 3.58 MHz and 4.1 MHz.

Using a monitor of bandwidth known to be flat far higher than these frequencies, the display will then quickly indicate the system's frequency capabilities. The burst wherever you cannot differentiate the white from the black vertical lines is the bandwidth maximum of your system. Fig. 20-3B is a waveform display of the multiburst. Note that the waveform monitor shows a slight falling off of linearity at the higher frequencies (wedge-shaped instead of rectangular-shaped display). It is not recommended that multiburst be used by cable subscribers for they may very well end up blaming the cablecaster for their receivers'

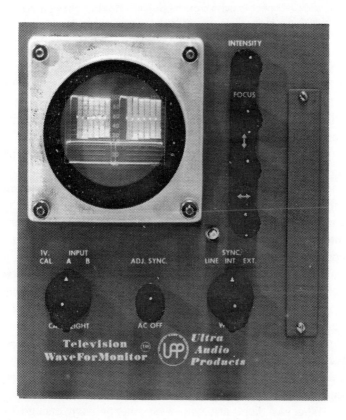

Fig. 20-3B. Waveform monitor display of multiburst. Note slight high-frequency roll-off creating wedge pattern. (Courtesy Ultra Audio Products.)

Fig. 20-4. Waveform and picture display of ten-step staircase pattern. Video monitor in pulse cross mode shifts display, shows horizontal blanking and equalizing pulses from the sync generator.

bandwidth limitations. Figure 20-4 shows both waveform and picture display of the previously described step pattern.

The waveform monitor is your best friend in the television studio. It tells you things that a video-level meter either cannot reveal or discloses very inaccurately. Quick confirmation of this may easily be achieved by setting a camera's iris or target control to *automatic* and observing picture quality (on your color monitor) and output level (on your waveform monitor). Compare your waveform monitor's indication with that of the meter on the camera-control unit. Most likely their indications of picture intensity will be quite divergent. Then, turn the camera's control to MANUAL. You will no doubt be able to manually improve picture quality to a very noticeable degree—as observed on your color monitor and in reliance upon your waveform monitor. In addition, the WFM will display picture disturbances and spikes, not shown on any meter, sync-pulse intensity, some scene-lighting deficiencies, picture strength in each portion of the scene and, of course, *true* video-output level of the camera, program line or video tape recorder to which it is connected.

Whereas there are now WFMs inexpensive enough to permit you to buy one with each camera and another for the program line, you may wish to augment them with one of the more costly units that is capable of displaying Vertical

Interval Test Signals (VITS). One of the niceties of television is that it permits system testing during program transmission without interference. The networks are virtually always transmitting VITS, and many local stations transmit them via their microwave from studio to transmitter to test transmitter quality (as received back at the studio). These VITS are available to you, the cableman. Use them! They are customarily transmitted simultaneously on lines 18 and 19 of the *odd* fields, and also on the same lines of the *even* fields. Furthermore, there is nothing to prevent transmssion on lines 16 through 21—or any of the first 21 lines which comprise the vertical-blanking interval. (These lines are not displayed on the TV screen.)

A WFM equipped for VITS display permits you to select any line, from 16 to 21, of either field, and to see what is being transmitted at those times. You will be amazed to see multiburst, sine-square pulse, "window," staircase, 2T bar, 12.5T bar, and (oh, my gosh) VIR signal. To prevent these innumerable simultaneous tests (inserted by an inexpensive VITS inserter device) from "splattering" into the program area they are transmitted at reduced intensities. Let's look at some of them.

Instead of full-intensity transmission, the multiburst usually consists of a 100 IRE-unit burst flag, while the multiple bursts are at only 70 IRE intensity. You might look for this on line 18 of field one. On the corresponding line in field two, you should expect to see color bars saturated 100% but only of 75% amplitude. Now, if at the same time you were to look at line 19 field one, you may see the ever present color-reference burst plus a modulated five-riser staircase followed by 2T sine-squared bar (0.25 microsecond duration) followed by 12.5T modulated sine-square pulse (1.571 microseconds), all this preceding 18 microseconds of white ("window") at full level. The *modulated* staircase can measure burst-phase errors in stabilizers and clampers, plus incorrect white-clip level. The 2T-pulse is useful in checking frequency response by comparing its height with the height of the window, but this is usable only in response to 3 MHz. Beyond this frequency, we must use the 12.5T pulse as we enter the "chrominance area" to check relative chrominance/luminance gain and delay which cause saturation errors and color-registration problems. Delay distortion, such as observed when colors "bleed" to the right side of the screen, means chrominance delay—and color misregistration.

The 18 microseconds of bar signal is under the control of a 2T sine-squared filter. If it is undistorted the system can be deemed free of tilt (low-frequency distortion), smear, and streaking. There is a special graticule useful in checking 2T and 18-microsecond signals. It is called the K graticule and, in the case of the former pulse, it allows comparison of the rise and fall times of the 2T-pulse against the gradations printed on the K-factor scale. If the slope(s) of the pulse does not parallel the printed slope, meaning the rise and fall times are not symmetrical, quadrature distortion is present.

Truly, the waveform monitor is your best friend—and your best investment. Here's food for thought: One of the reasons that multiburst is transmitted in both fields during VITS-casting is that, if it were inserted in only one of the two fields, certain receivers might show *flicker*—very low-frequency fluctuations—because of AGC-level changes from field to field (30 Hz).

To conclude Part 1, let's return to VIRS—Vertical-Interval Reference Signal—which is proposed to be transmitted on line 20, both fields. It consists of the customary 12 microseconds of horizontal blanking with color burst. Then the reference signals begin: 24 microseconds of 3.579545 MHz at zero-degrees phase (the same as the color burst should be) and with 40 IRE units of amplitude, but beginning at the luminance reference point on the graticule (50 IRE, known as "Y-level"). To put it another way, the chrominance reference bar is of 40 IRE amplitude modulation and is generated at the 70 IRE level. Equipment in the system that shifts the phase relationship of color sync and chroma-bar will be exposed via the VIRS by comparing the burst phase of these two.

Next follows 12 microseconds of Y-level at 50 IRE

intensity. Now, if the chroma bar is not sitting precisely at this Y-level point, the luminance/chrominance relationship is upset and must be corrected. Finally we observe 12 microseconds of black-reference (7.5 IRE) level, and with this at 7.5 and luminance-bar at 50, the luminance level is normal. Added to all this is 3.5 microseconds of "front porch" going into horizontal blanking and we have the total time of one TV line—63.5 microseconds. In closing it must be pointed out that distortions observed via the VITS may be caused by the television station's and not the cablecaster's equipment. But you won't know it until you've compared various stations as seen on your system.

The next chapter covers, among other things, all the equipment you need for studio-equipment repair and maintenance—and the way to go about it.

# Chapter 21

# Color Teleproduction Center—
# Test Instrumentation

In the immediately preceding chapter of this book, we described how you would use your staircase generator, multiburst generator, and color bars for set up of your studio monitors, both color and monochrome. We showed how the CATV operator could use this equipment to benefit his subscribers too. Finally, we showed how the virtually ever-present VITS (Vertical Interval Test Signals) being transmitted by commercial television stations can be used for checking CATV distribution quailty.

In mentioning VITS, I would like to recommend that you consider feeding them through your studio equipment. After all, these test signals—particularly the 2T bar and 18-microsecond "window" constantly broadcast as VITS—are available to you without your having to pay for them! And did you know that you can buy your own VITS encoders which accept feeds from your test-signal generators and put them on any desired line(s) during the 21-line vertical interval? They're expensive, but may be very helpful to the sophisticated CATV operation where continual testing of distribution equipment is undertaken.

## Calibrating Color Monitors

From time to time during this book we've emphasized the fact that the most important thing you can do in your studio is to calibrate and match your monitors—particularly the color units. Without this, not only may your color cameras *never* be matched, but probably they will never be delivering true color fidelity, especially from day to day—or even throughout any given day. Then, of course, there is the registration and calibration of the cameras themselves. Whereas most of the equipment we will recommend is for maintenance of the overall system and repair of the various equipment that make up your complete studio, two units devoted to monitor and camera calibration, respectively, deserve our attention.

The IRT Mark II monitor comparator, Fig. 21-1, offers extra-fast precise setup of color monitors. It requires a staircase or window pattern to be displayed on the monitor being set up. It is handheld or tripod mountable and is unaffected by average ambient light, colors, or other monitors. Simply, the IRT generates a light source and lets you compare it with the light output of your monitor. A built-in neutral wedge filter facilitates setup of 19 ft.-Lamberts (ft.L.) (peak white) with the proposed international "illuminant D" (D 6500°K) standard color-temperature for color monitors. It also provides a 0.95 ft-L *low-light* reference, for which you adjust screen brightness and gain (contrast) appropriately.

### Checking Cameras

For your cameras, the "Porta-Pattern," Fig. 21-2 consists of a metal frame (mountable on a standard microphone stand or may be used as an easel) enclosing four separate hard-backed 9 × 12-in. charts of standard resolution, linearity, registration, and logarithmic reflectance. Included are Munsell chips with black nonreflective cloth. After using a chart, pull it out, place it behind the others, and make your appropriate camera

Fig. 21-1. Unique compact device permits quick brightness and contrast settings of color monitors displaying appropriate test pattern. (Courtesy Television Equipment Associates.)

Fig. 21-2. Rugged portable chartbox contains all patterns needed for camera alignment and matching. (Courtesy Telecommunications Industries, Ltd.)

adjustments with the next chart, and so forth. Keep the chartbox just off-stage, but still under your scene lighting, and you'll be able to make quick camera corrections under actual set-lighting conditions during a show by turning a camera temporarily toward the Porta-Pattern. These two accessories will prove to be necessities before long, and will become invaluable as you follow the manufacturer's recommendations for camera setup.

### Think About Leaving Equipment Switches "On"

We turn now to one of the most perplexing of problems—whether or not to turn off your studio equipment after each use. If your studio is to be used daily, leave everything "on" (except for motors of any kind, of course). Color cameras, in particular, require considerable warmup, and even after you've waited the required time specified by the manufacturer, then made your setup, you'll still have to recalibrate, no doubt. Never turning off the cameras (nor the sync generator and pulse-distribution amplifiers) will serve to minimize your setup efforts. But, solid-state power supplies, without "crowbar" protection against voltage runaway due to regulator failure, could damage much of your equipment while nobody is watching; and failure of a camera's sweep circuits could cause costly damage—even to other cameras if you've neglected to isolate the sweeps via pulse distribution amplifiers (and there are three tubes you can "lose" in each of the color cameras, in most instances).

Remember that the single fuse in a power supply protects only the power transformer. It will not shut down the power supply if it loses dc voltage regulation! And with loss of regulation, output voltage could double. Therefore, you will have to decide for yourself whether the advantages in quicker setup, greater stability, and longer equipment life are worth the danger of leaving the equipment on for long periods during which it will be unattended. In our building, we never leave fluorescent lights on unattended because we've had ballasts catch fire on two occasions. We install crowbar circuits on certain power supplies. We have a spare plug-in power supply for all our distribution amplifiers—and, of course, spare DAs—because we'd be down-and-out without them. We also have two sync generators—the heart of the video system—plus a changeover device and another sync generator in Maintenance. Finally, we have a backup video switcher, normally used in the Telecine/VTR room which can be substituted for our primary switcher in dire emergency.

## Testing Your Sync Generator

For those who are able to receive broadcasts from a network "O&O" station, here's a slick way to test the accuracy of your sync generator: Receive a program, a network feed, from the station, and view it on a monitor equipped to accept external sync input. Feed sync to it from your sync generator and switch from internal to external sync. If your picture does not roll, your sync generator is excellent. In effect, what you're doing is comparing your sync generator's stability with that of a rubidium standard at network headquarters in New York, a reference second only in accuracy to that of the National Bureau of Standards. You will never find anything more precise than this beautiful service provided gratis by the three "nets." Incidentally, most of the time, the O&O's are genlocked to New York even when not transmitting a network feed; but the independent network affiliates cannot be counted on for this.

## A Full Complement of Equipment

Figure 21-3 proposes an elaborate list of the equipment an advanced teleproduction color facility would have for

| Equipment | Manufacturer or Distributor |
|---|---|
| Camera setup charts | Telecommunications Industries Ltd. |
| Color comparator | Television Equipment Associates |
| Pulse-cross Monitor | Ultra Audio Products |
| Waveform monitor with line selection | Tektronix |
| Electronic AC voltmeter | Hewlett-Packard |
| Electronic DC voltmeter | Hewlett-Packard |
| 10 MHz oscilloscope | Leader Instruments |
| Audio oscillator | General Radio |
| VITS encoder/decoder | TeleMation |
| VITS generator | Tektronix |
| Capacitor analyzer | Sprague |
| Transistor checker (in-circuit) | B&K |
| V-O-M | Simpson; Triplett |
| Staircase ("step") generator | Telemet/Geotel; Riker |
| Multiburst generator | Telemet/Geotel; Riker |
| Color sync generator, EIA | Lenco; Shibaden |
| Hi-fi monitor, amplifier & loudspeaker | Acoustic Research |
| NTSC vectorscope | Ultra Audio Products |
| Precision color monitor | World Video |
| Audio recorder alignment tapes | Ampex |
| Telecine test films and slides | SMPTE |
| TV demodulator (tuner), all channel | Dynair |

Fig. 21-3. Test equipment for use in the maintenance room and/or color studio.

setup, calibration, and maintenance of all studio equipment. Representative manufacturers of the recommended equipment are also shown. This array is not for the faint of heart, for the cost could be in the $7500 range and even much higher. Some of the items are necessities; others are not. Some equipment belongs in the studio; other pieces go on your service bench. A good idea is to feed mixed (composite) sync to a terminated jack in the maintenance area from your studio, saving the cost of another sync generator. You should also have a spare coax to carry test signals from your studio (burst, step, bars) to Maintenance for the repairman's use. Or, have all test generators in Maintenance, and feed them to the studio as needed. (But, don't forget to take them with you on "remotes!")

The list of recommendations is not truly complete in that I've omitted the color-bar generator (because your camera's encoder contains one) and a sine/square and window-pattern generator (because VITS will give you this). You may want to include other items your own experience has shown to be worthwhile; and of course I have not included any of the specialized additional equipment needed for CATV transmission-line quality checks.

Want to generate your own VITS? Well, if having VITS constantly on the line proves to be of value to you, why not create your own? By including a VITS encoder in your program line, then feeding the desired test signals into the encoder, they'll be constantly available for CATV transmission-line testing. The encoder lets you put your test signal on any one of about eight lines in the vertical interval. With additional encoders you can put VITS on various lines simultaneously. (Refer to detailed discussion of Vertical Interval Test Signals in the preceding chapter.) Of course, you must observe the modulation limits for Vertical-Interval transmission; and in order to generate all of the useful signals, you should procure a test-signal generator designed especially for use in VITS transmission. Your investment in test equipment is dictated by the extent and nature of the testing you must do, the government requirements, your commitment to your customers and the degree of your dedication to technical perfection—tempered, of course, by the weight of your pocketbook.

One of the most worthwhile things you can do, especially if you're not located near a major city, is to send your chief engineer (yourself?) to one of the helical video tape recorder maintenance schools, such as those operated by Sony and Ampex. These quickie courses, usually lasting three days, are marvelous (even if you're a very experienced "First Phone ticketholder") and help you to troubleshoot your helical VTR in very quick order so that you can get it back into service promptly and inexpensively. Contact your nearest authorized dealer for details—even if you don't use one of the brands of equipment mentioned.

# Chapter 22

# Make Film & Fones
# Work For You

As was brought home at a just-concluded recent NCTA convention, there are often better ways for the cableman to cablecast than with videotapes he makes himself or obtains from outside sources. Do you have the staff, the studio, the equipment, and the production money to produce your own shows? Are you essentially limited to interviews and low-budget settings? Is your video tape recorder not reproducing broadcast-grade sync pulses? Is your live-camera color quality disappointing? Do you have color? If the answers you give yourself bring tears to your eyes, consider one potent alternative—film!

Recent, or even not-so-recent, feature films may have to be ruled out because the nearby commercial stations have long ago gobbled up rights to the libraries. And there are 16mm prints in distributors' hands not available for rent for telecasting until after theatrical showings. But do investigate this possibility. There are film buyers to serve you and there are innumerable lavishly produced educational films, travelogues, governmental films (domestic and foreign), that are interesting, informative, and downright entertaining, available virtually free of charge—and begging for exhibition.

In lining up films, don't overlook the efforts of the college student filmmakers. Consider also appealing to the amateur photographers in your audience to bring you their best efforts. Why not schedule this as a regular feature—simultaneously improving your public relations and performing a public service. Invite amateurs to become "staff reporters" and shoot color slides of newsworthy events, while making an audio tape to run as a voice-over to these slides. With a press-card from your CATV system in their pockets, they'll "break their necks" to do you justice—especially when you run a slide that gives the all-important on-the-air credit. (Remember, photography is the nation's number one hobby.)

Yes, in spite of anything you may have heard or preconceived, film is often quicker, easier, and cheaper than videotape. What about the cost and delays in processing, you ask? Well, for news slides shoot 35mm *monochrome reversal* film, and the photographer can process it in minutes. For feature stories or news of less than immediate nature, shoot color and have it back from the lab in 48 hours or less. Find a way to solve the problem instead of using it as an excuse not to proceed.

Technically, film (motion or still) usually avoids the problems encountered with inexpensive color television cameras or inexperienced crews. And it always avoids the dilemma of the abominable sync stability found in most of the helical VTRs—to say nothing of the lack of real interchangeablility of videotapes (even *quadruplex*!) and the inherent problems of noise, dropouts, stretch, flagging. lockup time, color rendition, and level changes—even with tapes played on the VTR that made them. Most of the series appearing week-in-and-week-out in network or network-affiliated television, and most of the features shot by the "nets" for television are shot on film—35mm motion picture film, at that. So let's not rush to rule out any form of film just because we've entered the magical world of electronic pictures. And don't overlook the possibility of using your film chain as a film and/or slides-to-videotape transfer service. There are businesses and educational enterprises who might be grateful for the availability of such a service.

**Understand the Film Island**

To get the most from our Telecine operation we must consider the characteristics and limitations of our *film island*. First of all, recognize that motion picture film must be reversed, otherwise it will appear backwards on television. This is because the film is designed to be

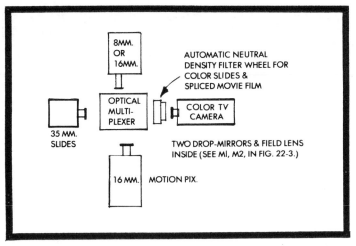

Fig. 22-1. Equipment placement for complete three-source film island.

The figure labels read:

8MM. OR 16MM.

AUTOMATIC NEUTRAL DENSITY FILTER WHEEL FOR COLOR SLIDES & SPLICED MOVIE FILM

OPTICAL MULTI-PLEXER

COLOR TV CAMERA

35 MM. SLIDES

TWO DROP-MIRRORS & FIELD LENS INSIDE (SEE MI, M2, IN FIG. 22-3.)

16 MM. MOTION PIX.

projected onto a screen and not into the viewer's (or camera's) eye. This reversal is accomplished via a mirror in the telecine optical system. Obviously, there must be an odd number of mirrors to project movie film; i.e., one, three, or (hopefully not as many as) five. Slides also require reversing. In this instance, just reverse them in the slideholder and project them straight into the TV camera. Figure 22-1 shows the layout of a standard optical multiplexer.

The curse of all low-cost units is that there is no failure protection and there is no provision to preview any film while another is on-the-air. If your telecine (T/C) camera fails, you must have another complete film chain on hand. Also, the T/C-man may be unable to precheck his cine film status prior to airing (because the chain is in use) and the video operator has no way of seeing if the film is properly cued or if the correct slide is in proper position.

Commercial broadcasters solve these problems by having a number of film chains, and the networks often dispense with multiplexers and have each movie projector directly feeding its own camera (with optical-image reversal added, of course). One manufacturer of fine but modestly priced film islands has just introduced a unique compromise for this problem by adding a number of mirrors to his basic telecine system. The result of this, Fig. 22-2, is a four-in, two-out film island permitting the feeding of two slide projectors and two film projectors to either of two television cameras. It is immediately evident that one camera can preview anything while the other is showing something else. And should a camera fail, the same projectors are ready to feed the other camera instantly.

Compare how this is accomplished, Fig. 22-2, with the single-camera system of Fig. 22-1. Note that the two-camera multiplexer permits all projectors to be on at any time (without interference) and, most importantly, that with this system it is not necessary ever to optically pass through an unwanted source to get to the desired one. True, this two-camera system is expensive, but far less so, and less bulky, than two independent film islands. It is also

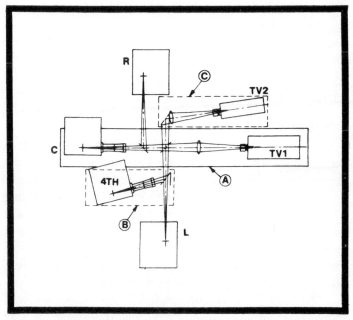

Fig. 22-2. Shows projection path. Indicated are: **A**, two drop mirrors on center for changeover; **B**, fourth input, slides, shares with left movie projector, is dormant when movie is in use, with camera; **R**, right-hand movie unit takes one or three mirrors, depending on camera fed. (Courtesy Zei-Mark Corp. Photo by Don Lauritzen.)

Fig. 22-3. Four-in, two-out film island (one of the movie projectors and the two slide projectors are visible). Island allows operator to preview one source while airing a second; and it allows rapid fill-in if one camera fails. (Courtesy Zei-Mark Corp. Photo by Don Laurtizen.)

more versatile. If you plan to put film on the air, plan to expand to this system as soon as your volume warrants it.

### Use an Interfone System

You may wish to accompany your T/C operation with a paging system if T/C is located in a room separate from the control room. I heartily recommend putting all mechanical (noisy) apparatus in a separate room. This means T/C and VTR; but your space, budget and personnel limitations will make this decision for you. If T/C is isolated, be sure it includes an interfone station for the T/C man; and since he may not always have his headset on, many broadcasters have a loudspeaker system for paging Telecine.

The interfone system included on most low-cost cameras is woefully inadequate. We could overlook the poor quality if we could get enough intensity. The latter is particularly a problem on sports remotes, long camera cable runs or in talking to areas of high noise such as Telecine is liable to be. Figure 22-4 shows a separate

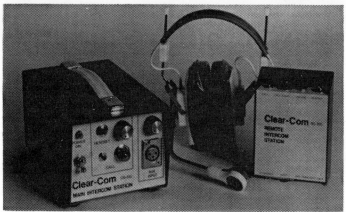

Fig. 22-4. High-intensity interfone can feed a PA system or accept program audio, or both.

interfone system which could be incorporated into your cameras' intercom provided you have wires available, one of which must be shielded. In this system, the audio is actually a dynamic microphone's output carried on single-conductor shielded wire. Each headset has its own amplifier with one master station required per system of up to 30 stations. The unshielded wire carries power to each station.

You can loop from one station to the next. You can feed the intercom to a paging system. There's a call light to attract the operator's attention if he's away from his phone. High voice quality, rather than telephone quality, is provided and noise-cancelling microphones are used. The lightweight remote stations may be attached to the user's belt, and the earphones are infinitely more comfortable than the customary telephone operator's headset. These reasonably priced interfones are a worthy addition to your live and film intercommunication lash-up.

# Chapter 23

# Good Studio Practices

The preceding chapters of this book run the gamut of architecture, mobile units, audio, video, lighting, electrical installations, and maintenance. We've covered many practical points in the process, but perhaps the time has arrived to recap a few rules of good practice and pitfalls to avoid. However, be mindful of the fact that certain rules must be bent where it is necessary to conserve space, improve portability or mobility, and of course for cost considerations.

First of all, forget that control-room window. This is a wasteful and needless carryover from the disc-recording industry. In television, survey your studio via an inexpensive surveillance camera and monitor, because all the money you spend on glass, soundproofing, and moistureproofing will be wasted when your window gets blocked with personnel, drapes, props, sets, and cameras. Don't waste your money on fancy acoustic tile as is found in recording studios. Soundstages are never pretty—and are not expected to be. "Live" (reverberant) rooms can be deadened through the installation of velvet drapes which are highly sound absorbent and may often be bought used from theatre supply houses. Wallboard, properly installed with rockwool separations, is excellent for sound isolation.

Don't forget, sound goes both ways—in and out. If you contemplate high sound levels, such as that generated by musical groups, a few hundred dollars spent on an acoustics consultant will reap you great rewards by preventing misspent dollars and hours of regret. Hopefully, your studio will be at least 15 ft high. Be sure to provide dressing rooms and a lavatory for the actors. An intercom between control and dressing rooms is handy.

Don't invest in that glamorous mobile unit unless you're sure you'll be doing a multitude of remotes. A van sitting idle most of the time is a waste of thousands of dollars. Instead, think about renting a truck, as needed, and putting your studio equipment in it. When you get to your destination you may be better off taking all the control equipment out and moving it as close as possible to the action—unless you want to spend thousands of extra dollars on heavy but delicate color-camera cables—and the men to pull them. Remember, too, that when your van has to be serviced, all that valuable delicate equipment is stuck in it, to be stolen or damaged. When you go on remotes, bring a couple of good flashlights (one will always fail, you know), as many hand tools as possible, a VOM, and be prepared for the fact that there may not be adequate power from a single outlet to run all your equipment, particularly color equipment.

Meanwhile, back at the studio: Contrary to recording studios, many video plants have wiring brought into the equipment racks from the top. This is usually more convenient and cheaper than floor-flush ducting. Shelves

You don't need a control room window; use instead a surveillance camera. (Courtesy Telaudio Centre. Photo by Don Lauritzen.)

should be constructed along appropriate walls. Professional cable trays even have upward, downward, and sideway bends to gently guide the cables in the directions desired. Ac wiring must be spaced away from audio and video lines to prevent hum radiation. Although video levels are essentially the same (1V) in all portions of the system, audio program lines are about 60 dB higher in level than microphone lines. Audio lines of 40 dB or more difference in level should be spaced apart to prevent crosstalk. All long audio lines should be two-conductor shielded wires, otherwise you'll lose high-frequency response utilizing high-impedance microphone lines. You may have to make input and output adapter boxes incorporating transformers of appropriate impedance to match the helical-recorder input and output circuits to your properly designed audio-mixing system.

And don't make audio an *also ran*. It is penny-wise and pound-foolish to skimp on audio because you've spent your money on the video. Your audio should include a minimum of four microphone inputs, record-turntable input, and feeds to and from a professional two-track audio recorder, plus the ability to accept other high-level sources, such as telecine audio and VTR audio playback. You must also provide for playback of videotaped audio to the actors in the studio; possibly prerecorded audio tapes and discs too. Will an announcer or bandleader need to hear program audio or special playback for cue purposes? Will you need a reverb machine? How about an equalizer or filter for special audio effects? Don't forget provision for the director or vision mixer or audioman to page the stage. Just as you'll want an intercom to the dressing rooms, you'll also want one on the stage. This has no connection with the headsets used by the crew.

Similarly, you'll want intercom in Telecine. Telecine? By all means. Plan on a separate soundproofed Telecine/VTR room. If you don't isolate all the noisemaking equipment (motors) you'll find control-room operations terribly nerve-wracking, much to the detriment of production quality—and budget. If you can afford it, use a film island with three or four inputs and two outputs, which allows you to preview one source while another is in SHOW mode. Remote telecine control from the control room will facilitate smoother productions. If your budget can stand it, put your audio equipment in a separate room and give the audioman preview, program, and surveillance monitors. You may then have to provide paging to Audio as well as the Stage, not to mention Telecine. All this depends on how sophisticated and broadcast-oriented your teleplant is to be. Careful wiring practices to avoid ground loops must be observed. One rule is that the shields of balanced audio lines should be grounded at the receiving end only. But in elaborate multistudio layouts, shields are usually compelled to be grounded at both ends in rack-to-rack wiring. But then all racks must be firmly bolted to a substantially solid ground.

Watch out for those local electrical codes as far as your stage lighting array is concerned. One way to minimize harassment from city electrical and fire inspectors is to use as much portable cordage as possible. To be truly portable your luminaires' cables must have plugs at the "cold" end, rendering them fully disconnectable from the power source. This also permits you to patch any light to any dim or nondim circuit, thus increasing flexibility and minimizing the number of luminaires required. Your focusing spotlights should always be equipped with Fresnel lenses, otherwise they'll be terribly uncontrollable. Carefully review lamp-life and efficiency tables and plan on 3000°K usable color temperatures rather than marrying yourself to the costly and unnecessary 3200°K "rule." Keep all lights suspended from the rigging and, if possible, none on the floor.

You'll need a precision monitor and a device for calibrating it, otherwise your final camera color will vary from day-to-day and operator-to-operator. Monitors incorporating hue and saturation controls cannot be used for setup, but may be compared with the color rendition of the precision monitor. Obtain a set of color camera registration and associated charts, plus similar slides and films for Telecine. Use control-room lighting that has no effect on the hue of the color monitors. The special-effects section of your video switcher should be used in split-screen mode to make final camera color comparisons. Cameras should be allowed to warm-up and settle down for at least a half-hour, preferably double that, before your attempting any adjustments. Calibrate your monitor before you camera.

Clean all heads of the video tape recorder before each day's use—more often, if possible. Clean pinchwheels and guides with appropriate fluids just as often. (Purchase a VTR that's at least as expensive as your most costly color camera—a good rule of thumb.) Use as high a grade of videotape as you can afford. In this way you'll experience fewer dropouts, less head clogging, tape damage, and head wear. Add a dropout compensator to all color machines not equipped with one and always check VTR playback quality with a pulse cross monitor, "tweaking" the machine to optimize its playback. Try to use a time-base corrector on all tapes being aired or dubbed. Never rely on meters for setting video levels. The waveform monitor is the only accurate indicator. Use only an RS-170 NTSC sync generator. Units with the valuable genlock feature are now relatively inexpensive. Store tapes at a temperature no higher than 70° and at about 45% humidity.

All monochrome monitors should include dc-restoration circuitry, which may be inexpensively added to most units. This will generate truer and blacker blacks and whiter whites. Use a ten-step staircase generator to set brightness and contrast on all monitors. In the absence of such a generator, train a camera on a precision staircase-camera chart and feed it to all monitors. Although video patching is costly, a well thought-out patchbay will facilitate a world of quick and easy testing and temporary hookups and circuit changes—provided your studio is more than just an array of tabletop equipment. Whereas sloping turrets are glamorous, they are very wasteful of space and also not all they're cracked up to be as far as human engineering is concerned. Consider standard vertical racks with the possible inclusion of a desktop.

# Index